PRAISE FOR *PEOPLE OVER PROFIT*

People Over Profit is a fresh look at timeless and important values that have always inspired leaders in the marketplace. Dale's work may challenge you to completely rethink your business.

—SCOTT HARRISON, CEO AND FOUNDER, CHARITY: WATER

"Leaders like Dale are changing the very definition of the word *entrepreneur*. I've spent years personally learning the lessons inside this book from Dale. I'm glad you'll have the same chance now too!"

**—JON ACUFF, *NEW YORK TIMES*
BEST-SELLING AUTHOR OF *START***

"Dale recognized that to fix big problems we need to ask big questions. His solutions are not only exciting but practical and powerful. This is a must read for every aspiring entrepreneur."

**—ADAM BRAUN, *NEW YORK TIMES* BEST-SELLING
AUTHOR AND FOUNDER OF PENCILS OF PROMISE**

"*People Over Profit* espouses the biggest, best idea of our generation: we need a new breed of entrepreneur—an honest, loving, generous, and authentic one. This book shows us how to get there."

**—CLAIRE DIA ORTIZ, MANAGER OF SOCIAL
INNOVATION AT TWITTER**

"*People Over Profit* is not just a big idea; it's the only idea. And while everyone is searching for a quick fix for their business, Dale has outlined a true fix. Value people and you will win."

—JASON RUSSEL, FOUNDER OF INVISIBLE CHILDREN

"No marketing strategy or business tactic will ever surpass the power of caring for people. What Dale uncovers here is the secret to every outrageously successful company."

—JOHNNY EARLE, FOUNDER OF JOHNNY CUPCAKES

"*People Over Profit* uncovers the true fabric that separates good and bad, greed and giving, and selfish and selfless. These words should be the backbone of every business leader in our world."

—MIKE FOSTER, FOUNDER OF PEOPLE OF THE SECOND CHANCE

"Entrepreneurs . . . listen up. Stop chasing tactics and strategies and start leading with heart and empathy. It's the findings here in Dale's philosophy that will surely become your secret weapon."

—LEWIS HOWES, FOUNDER OF *THE SCHOOL OF GREATNESS* PODCAST

PEOPLE
OVER
PROFIT

PEOPLE OVER PROFIT

BREAK THE SYSTEM. LIVE WITH PURPOSE.
BE MORE SUCCESSFUL.

DALE PARTRIDGE

NELSON
BOOKS

An Imprint of Thomas Nelson

Published in Nashville, Tennessee, by Nelson Books, an imprint of Thomas Nelson. Nelson Books and Thomas Nelson are registered trademarks of HarperCollins Christian Publishing, Inc.

Author is represented by literary agent Christopher Ferebee, 2834 Hamner Avenue, Suite 456, Norco, California 92860.

Thomas Nelson, Inc., titles may be purchased in bulk for educational, business, fund-raising, or sales promotional use. For information, please e-mail SpecialMarkets@ThomasNelson.com.

IE: 978-0-7180-3620-1

Library of Congress Cataloging-in-Publication Data

Partridge, Dale, 1985–
  People over profit : break the system, live with purpose, be more successful / Dale Partridge.
    pages cm
  Includes bibliographical references.
  ISBN 978-0-7180-2174-0
1. Management--Social aspects. 2. Corporate culture. 3. Organizational behavior. 4. Business ethics. 5. Social responsibility of business. I. Title.
  HD31.P3135 2015
  658.4'08--dc23   2014032495

Printed in the United States of America

15 16 17 18 19 RRD 6 5 4 3 2 1

TO VERONICA,
MY WIFE, MY FRIEND, MY ROCK.
YOUR NEVER-ENDING SUPPORT OF MY DREAMS
CAPTURES MY HEART AND MAKES ME WHOLE.

CONTENTS

WITH UNDERSTANDING COMES CHANGE 55

BREAK THE SYSTEM FOR "GOOD" 155

FOREWORD

In today's ever-changing business world, the idea of "people over profit" might be one of the easiest things to say but one of the hardest things to actually do. Yet in the right hands and from the right heart—such as Dale's—the words in this book can become incredibly powerful and galvanizing. They can inspire employees and customers and communities to join together and not only want more out of their professional and personal lives but want to *do more*. And when that happens, people can change the world.

Still, to have real impact and to make a lasting impression in hearts, minds, and bottom lines, all businesses, whether they're cause-based or not, must go beyond words and have their ideals and ideas turned into constant, passionate, and relentless action. I believe Dale has proven his ability to lead such a movement, and this certainly has been shown through his recent entrepreneurial efforts. But the idea of conscious capitalism, and the democracy of that idea, proves that it can do so much more.

The beauty and brilliance of what Dale strives to achieve day in and day out, and what he has written about here, combine some of the most powerful and time-resistant business ethos—such as quality, authenticity, and transparency—with other essentials that resonate much deeper. *Truth, generosity*, and *courage* are not and cannot simply be buzzwords in today's business world. They must be at the core. And they must be sent forth into the world by people who passionately believe in these ideals.

Much like TOMS, what Dale is encouraging is unique to our time and place and generation. Thanks to technology, many of the old rules of business no longer apply, or are being rewritten daily, weekly, and monthly. What's amazing to see is that more often than not, today's countless social entrepreneurs are sidestepping them altogether. They are people, after all, and their influence is immense.

It's an exciting time. It's real, it's not going away, and it's only going to get bigger, braver, and better with people like Dale Partridge helping to lead the way.

Carpe diem.

Blake Mycoskie
Founder of TOMS Shoes
New York Times best-selling author of
Start Something That Matters

In a time of universal deceit, telling the truth becomes a revolutionary act.

———

George Orwell

0

THE BRIGHT COUNTERPART

I've seen the same physician in Southern California for more than a decade, but somehow this visit felt different. Walking into the waiting room, I was greeted by a sterile scent and silence. Knowing the drill, I wrote my name on a clipboard with a plastic pen stamped with the name of a cholesterol pill. The receptionist didn't look up to acknowledge my presence, so after a few awkward moments trying to catch her eye, I took a seat.

Like most doctors' offices, there wasn't much to occupy one's attention. I could either stare at the tacky wallpaper or thumb through germ-covered magazines from 2009.

Squeezed into a stained, cloth chair and confined by eighteen sniffling and snotty people, I opted for the latter.

Three outdated magazines later, I looked at my watch to realize that I was forty-five minutes past my scheduled appointment time. My foot tapped nervously, and I shifted in my seat. Finally, a nurse popped her head out of the door: "Mr. Partridge." I rose and followed her down the hallway where she recorded my weight and temperature before dropping me off in a bleak room.

I waited again. This time, without even the benefit of a *Reader's Digest*. Finally, at one hour and twelve minutes past my appointment time, the physician arrived.

"Hello, Mr. Partridge," he said without looking up from my chart. "What can I help you with?"

I wanted to say he could help me by making me feel like I actually mattered, but I chose instead to explain that I had a killer case of heartburn.

"Oh, okay," he replied. "I'll give you a prescription of [some word that I think started with an X]. The nurse will get you taken care of."

And—boom—he was gone. Three minutes tops.

Gathering my things and collecting my prescription, I exited through the waiting room past a herd of patients en route to the same experience. In the parking lot that day, I sat in my car stunned at what had just transpired. I considered going back in and shouting, "What the heck is going on here?" and demanding an explanation for the antiquated, dishonoring experience and complete disregard for my time. With my luck, I figured that would probably end in being tackled or tasered by a four-hundred-pound man with the flu. So I let it go.

FEELINGS OF BETRAYAL

In retrospect, the outrage I felt that day is strange because I'd been through this exact scenario dozens, maybe hundreds, of times. I had only noticed what had always been there. In a recent study, 34 physicians were taped while serving more than 300 visits with patients. Those doctors spent an average of 1.3 minutes conveying crucial information about the patient's condition and treatment, and most of it was too technical for patients to grasp. Worse still, those same physicians thought they had spent more than 8 minutes. And this isn't just the doctors' fault. A few years ago, publicly traded HMOs began restricting doctors to a seven-minute "encounter" with each patient to keep shareholders happy. The industry is actually mandating lower quality in order to maximize profits.

Unfortunately, these kinds of experiences aren't restricted to health care. The last couple of decades have been dominated by companies and organizations that value profit more than the people they serve. From fashion to food, banking to advertising, we're confronted with examples of how ugly capitalism can be.

- Our grocery store shelves are packed with products from agricultural biotechnology companies who attack the purity of our food to increase efficiency even if it harms consumers.

- Cell-phone and satellite-dish companies force multi-year contracts on their customers, trapping them in a prison of subpar service where they must pay an expensive cancellation fee to switch to a superior competitor. This is apparently preferable to providing better products and services.

- Fast-food companies have increased efficiency at the expense of quality, creating menu items loaded with chemicals, preservatives, and thousands of calories that contribute to the obesity epidemic in America.

- Banks choose not to notify their customers or block transactions when customers hit a zero balance. Instead, they allow customers to borrow the money in multiple negative transactions per day while charging unmerciful overdraft fees. In 2012, consumers nationally paid $32 billion in overdraft fees, a $400 million jump from 2011.[1]

- Insurance companies reroute customers in predominantly English-speaking markets to an internationally outsourced customer support team where broken-English–speaking reps read from a rote script in hopes that a one-size-fits-all approach will somehow solve their individual problems.

When morality comes up against profit, it is seldom that profit loses.

———

Shirley Chisholm

#PeopleOverProfit

- Credit-card companies shell out hundreds of millions of dollars per year on positive marketing campaigns showcasing the rewards of using their product, but bury oppressive terms and conditions in the fine print. To convince you of their integrity, they offer you a small cash reward to refer a friend to sign up too.

All around us, colossal brands that once stood for integrity and quality have begun to tiptoe across ethical eggshells—condoning growth strategies, marketing campaigns, and customer-satisfaction policies that are not only unacceptable but also downright disingenuous—hoping their customers won't notice.

Unfortunately for them, customers have noticed, turning a corporate trend into a consumer-trust epidemic that has toppled more than one industry titan. The marketplace has given many deceptive companies a stark choice: change or die.

HOPE IS RISING

Luckily, change is afoot, and not just among existing organizations. In the midst of this downward capitalistic spiral, a bright counterpart is emerging. It's a counterpart that is healthy and contract free, that will pay more for better quality and higher ethical standards, that cares not just about profit but also the well-being of their customers and the state of the world. This bright counterpart has been called "conscious capitalism" or the "social good movement." But whatever label you choose, the trend is gaining serious traction.

According to a 2012 global survey, 47 percent of consumers now say they buy at least one brand that supports a good cause every month. To put this in perspective, that's a 47 percent increase since 2010. Additionally, 72 percent of consumers say they would recommend a brand that supports a good cause, which is a 38 percent increase since 2010.[2]

Take Panera Bread Company, for example. The sandwich chain has opened a handful of restaurants in urban areas where patrons pay only what they can afford. These "Panera Cares" restaurants have proven to be profitable, and the revenue generated is used to train at-risk kids.

And Panera is not alone. Fortune 500 companies are hiring personnel and forming new departments dedicated to giving back and promoting social responsibility. Organizations like Nordstrom, Southwest Airlines, and Trader Joe's are finding ways to pair social impact with solid business. Companies like Ben and Jerry's, known for giving away a portion of its profits to charity, and Whole Foods, which has made strong commitments to local community support, are thriving. And in recent years, start-ups like TOMS Shoes and Warby Parker came roaring into the marketplace with their revolutionary "one-for-one" model. That is, for every pair of TOMS shoes or Warby Parker glasses that a customer purchases, a pair is given to a person in need.

A few years ago, I began to notice the collision of capitalism's darker, deceptive side with the bright counterpart of the social good movement. And that's when I decided to plant my flag in the conversation by creating my company, Sevenly.

SKIN IN THE GAME

In February 2011, I was discussing the emerging business models focused on social good with my friend Aaron. He was a trailblazer in social media marketing, and his Facebook page had more than two million fans. Could we create an organization with a double bottom line—one that measured profitability and social impact? The idea seemed like a good one, but we didn't know where to start.

First of all, Aaron and I weren't just passionate about one particular cause. We saw many problems in the world that were begging for solutions. Second, we knew we weren't called to the field—to Africa or India or China or an impoverished neighborhood in urban America. But we did feel called to the people who were called to the field.

We began researching and found that more than 1.6 million charities existed in the United States. Of those, over 700 were going out of business every day.[3] The main reasons these charities were going under was lack of funding and lack of awareness. They had plenty of passion, but they needed help generating revenue and buzz. Off the top of our heads, Aaron and I could name only four charities each. When we asked our friends and families, they had the same problem.

What if we partnered with a different charity every week to help them raise funding and awareness? What if we created a social, good e-commerce company that partnered with a new charity every seven days? What if we created quality

I alone cannot change the world, but I can cast a stone across the waters to create many ripples.

———

Mother Teresa

products—clothing and art and jewelry—and for every item sold, we gave seven dollars to the week's charity?

At that moment, Sevenly was born.

Our first campaign was with International Justice Mission, raising funding and awareness to fight human trafficking in Southeast Asia. We partnered with Reese's Rainbow, working for the adoption of children with Down syndrome in Russia. We collaborated with Generosity Water to build clean-water wells in Haiti. We teamed up with Autism Speaks to fund speech therapy and unlock the voices of nonverbal children. Today, Sevenly has an incredible team, has generated millions in revenue, and has donated more than $4 million in $7 donations to charities across the world.

I've learned a lot from my work with Sevenly and from observing the other players in this bright counterpart. I believe these new business models represent the future—one we want and need to realize. I believe we can buy better and lead better and be better through committing to certain beliefs and practices in the marketplace. Together we can create a world even more wonderful than we might imagine.

PART 1

THE CYCLE WE'RE STUCK IN

Economists tell us that organizations are like people and weather; they operate in seasons. Most start small and passionate, the best ones grow, they all change, and many die.

Sociologists William Strauss and Neil Howe, in their book *The Fourth Turning*, argue that even America, "the great innovator," tends to think in linear terms. Like all of history, our culture runs in cycles, or "generational trends." Just below the surface is an underlying malady or an unseen rhythm, driven by forces that are easy to identify but only if one is willing to look hard enough.[1]

So what if the bright counterpart trends we're seeing aren't really new? What if they are as old as capitalism itself?

As Mark Twain has pointed out, "Nothing is older than America's habit of calling everything new."[2]

After creating Sevenly, I began to wonder, *Is what we're doing actually innovative? Is a corporation that authentically cares for people and desires to change the world a completely futuristic idea?* The answer is no. Absolutely not.

Then why have tens of thousands of organizations, over time, drifted away from their core values? It baffled me why so many companies would sacrifice their integrity and principles on the altar of efficiency and greed. Furthermore, I wondered why only a select few have been able to maintain their sense of identity and integrity, over decades of time, without compromise. What were they doing that nobody else was? What gave them the ability to not fall into the system?

I had never asked the deeper questions behind the trends I was seeing because, like many business leaders and entre-preneurs, I'm a problem solver. When I locate dysfunction, my first instinct is often to fix things that aren't working. Just ask my wife. Whenever a disagreement arises, she often grows irritated with the way I react. She wants to discuss the deeper issues, and I am searching for the shortest path to a solution.

Though the problem-solving impulse at its root is good, I often remind myself not to pursue it out of order. Humans are great at analyzing the *what*; our brains are built to think naturally in those terms. But in order to truly affect change, we must learn to address the *why* before we understand how to fix the *what*. When I looked at the organizational histories of America's most storied businesses, I discovered something fascinating: "bad" companies haven't always been bad. Even those organizations the media features in their annual collection of America's most hated companies did not start that way.

To demonstrate, look at the list of company names on the next page and mark next to them whether they strike you as bad or good in your mind.

What's interesting about this exercise is the organizations most people mark as bad companies were actually industry leaders in quality and customer service in their early years. And the companies that people mark as good are either in the early stages of their history or have worked to redeem their public image and internal practices in recent years. As

Vote for companies...

GOOD	or	BAD
☐	Wholefoods	☐
☐	Ford	☐
☐	Bank of America	☐
☐	Apple	☐
☐	AT&T	☐

it turns out, one's perception of a company often depends on when, in its history, the question is asked.

Perhaps the best example of this is the fast-food giant McDonald's. Founder Ray Kroc opened his first restaurant in the mid-1950s in Chicago, Illinois. The company motto was "Quality, Service, Cleanliness, and Value." Customers and employees were cherished, and even though the food arrived quickly, it was crafted with natural ingredients and quality in mind. No wonder the organization grew so rapidly.

But over time, efficiency began to trump quality and service. The marquee of quality was how many burgers were sold rather than how many were served well. In recent years, lawsuits were brought against the giant, which was constantly combating public scandals over the quality of everything from its hamburger patties to the manufacturing process used in their chicken nuggets.

Today, McDonald's is a notoriously low performer in the stock market. Some would say it has become known less for its aspirational principles than for high-speed delivery of low-cost products with negligible nutritional values. But it is telling that its public perception wasn't always so poor.

If a company is fortunate enough to last long enough—perhaps two or three generations—it may transform from having the perception of a good company to a bad company, and back again to being good. McDonald's is only one of a plethora of examples.

Upon surveying America's leading corporations throughout the last century, I've identified a cycle that America has been stuck in for centuries. Behind our capitalistic megamachine exists a pattern of corporate behavior, churning through seasons of honesty, efficiency, deception, and redemption. This cycle drives companies from a period where they value people over profit to a time when they value profit over people, and then back again. Within each era, certain values shift, drive, and change not only the business but also the marketplace as a whole.

4 Eras of Organizational Behavior

1. HONEST
2. EFFICIENT
3. DECEPTIVE
4. APOLOGETIC

If you look at most American organizations with a long enough history, you'll find this cycle dramatized in a striking way. Here are a few examples.

HONEST ERA

The Ford Motor Company was founded by Henry Ford on June 16, 1903. In a time before unions, when the average employee worked eighty to ninety hours per week, Ford became the first major organization in the world to offer a forty-hour workweek, employee health programs, and employee safety protections. In 1922, Edsel Ford, Henry's son and the company's president, explained that "Every man needs more than one day a week for rest and recreation. . . .

The Ford Company always has sought to promote [an] ideal home life for its employees. We believe that in order to live properly every man should have more time to spend with his family."[3]

EFFICIENT ERA

In 1955, Ford Motor Company had become known for large-scale manufacturing and management practices (known as Fordism). They still valued their workers and customers, but Ford had already begun shifting their focus to greater volume and efficiency. By the mid-twentieth century, Ford's high-capacity manufacturing practices paved the way for the Thunderbird and then the Mustang to become two of the top five most manufactured vehicles from sea to shining sea.

DECEPTIVE ERA

By the 1970s, Ford had seemingly abandoned many of their founding values. In 1971, Ford released the now-infamous Pinto, a subcompact car with deadly design flaws in its gas tank, causing it to often erupt in flames upon a rear-end collision. The car was named one of the "50 Worst Cars of All Time" by *Time* magazine because of its volatile nature and the notorious "Ford Pinto memo." The internal executive team calculated the cost of reinforcing the rear end at $121 million versus the estimated $50 million in payouts to victims. Even in the face of numerous deaths, Ford opted for the cheaper option of settling the resulting lawsuits rather than fixing the car.[4]

APOLOGETIC ERA

In the 1990s, Ford had recognized that internal problems had led to crippling public perceptions. They began investing in higher standards, which led to increased customer satisfaction and quality ratings for many vehicles. In 2009, when government bailout money was given to many American automobile manufacturers, Ford executives said, "Thanks, but no thanks." Instead, they released a series of national advertisements highlighting their determination to avoid bailout in an effort to regain consumer trust.

Unknown to most Ford executives and marketplace observers during that 106-year period, Ford Motor Company had cycled through the four eras of organizational behavior. They were unwittingly driven from a praiseworthy founding to decades of efficiency and greed, driven toward demise, and are now in a time of redemption and intentional return to their roots.

Organizations like Ford, and capitalism in general, follow this pattern in waves. For most organizations and business leaders, energy is invested in solving the current problems we're facing without stopping to diagnose where we are being driven from and to. Like a bad doctor, we treat the symptoms without diagnosing the disease.

So let's stop for a moment and perform a little checkup. Let's learn what each era actually looks like, so we can diagnose where we are, why we are there, and how we can make necessary changes to develop the organizations and marketplace we really want to create.

1

THE HONEST ERA

Captivated by Values

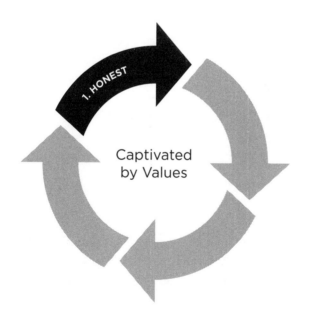

Imagine a company that is known for unbearably long checkout lines and poor customer service. They pay their workers low wages—so low, in fact, that many of them are forced to rely on Medicaid and food stamps to survive. Then picture this company with a CEO who makes more in an hour than most of his employees do all year. Imagine that this company has poorly run and understaffed stores filled with shelves stocked with goods produced overseas and often made by underpaid workers in inhumane conditions. And worse still, when they want to open a new store, they target rural communities, and once they've settled in, use predatory pricing to drive out small businesses. It is one of America's most hated companies.

Would you do business with such an organization?

No, of course not.

But the truth is, you and 245 million others do every single week.

But Walmart didn't start out this way.

Sam Walton was born in Kingfisher, Oklahoma, in 1918. He was the first son of a local banker, an Eagle Scout, avid hunter, and quarterback of his high school football team— the stereotypical "good ole' boy." Later he would serve as an army captain in World War II. In 1962, Walton birthed the first Walmart store in Rogers, Arkansas. His vision was to open as many large discount retail stores as possible in small, rural communities across the country. He was a strong leader and widely recognized as a man of integrity. Walton founded the organization on three basic beliefs: respect for the individual, service to customers, and striving for excellence. Undergirding it all was the commitment to "acting with integrity."[1]

Sam was known for job creation and paying his staff above industry standard. He demanded five-star customer satisfaction and encouraged Walmart "associates" to greet shoppers with a smile and always look them in the eye. Those associates who worked the hardest to capture and keep customers happy could expect limitless opportunities for advancement.

The plan worked, and three decades later, Walmart's stock was valued at $45 billion, and *Forbes* named Sam Walton the richest man in America. Even in the economic downturn of the early 1990s, the company thrived, increasing sales by more than 40 percent.[2]

As many of us have seen, Walmart's current practices have deviated from their founder's original vision. So there is a deeper lesson to be learned: no company starts out bad. Not even the ones we hate most. The question is, how did they get there?

WE ALL START CLEAN

When a company is first born, it is much like a human baby—pink-faced, innocent, existing almost exclusively for the benefit of others. Think about the start-up companies you know, and distill the common characteristics. Employees are excited. There's a clear mission and vision, usually focused around solving a problem or creating a better system or product. And, of course, every customer is considered critical.

No company starts out dirty, because they cannot afford to. They have to convince consumers they are worth their time and money. When you're an unknown entity, it's deadly to be recognized as unethical, impersonal, or misleading. As a result, your focus is the industrious pursuit of customer loyalty and your mission to create nothing short of an incredible and memorable experience.

The Honest Era is a time in a company's journey when mission, quality, and integrity live at the core of the organization. Their leaders are fanatically dedicated to improving not only the lives of their customers but their workforce too. They bring intense innovation to everything from marketing and customer support to their business model and even their supply chain. They are focused on the things that matter— employees, customers, and their brand. They fight for team buy-in at every level and celebrate even the smallest victories as a sign of progress toward a better world.

You see this in the recent boom of Internet-based companies launching from California's infamous Silicon Valley. Thousands of entrepreneurs are starting companies that redefine the definition of integrity in business, commerce, and capitalism as a whole.

Take, for instance, Airbnb.com, which has tipped the hotel

industry on its head by offering customers the ability to host and rent homes across the country. To top it off, they offer 24-7 customer support where real humans

THE HONEST ERA IS A TIME OF PEOPLE OVER PROFIT.

answer the phone. Combine that with incredible employee perks, such as $2,000 per year per employee for travel, a bring-your-dog-to-work option, free organic lunches, and complimentary health and fitness classes available almost around the clock. They have had incredible success in the marketplace, generating what could soon be $1 billion in annual revenue and renting more than 12 to 15 million rooms a night after only a few years in existence.[3]

The beautiful models of the Honest Era are naturally exceeding expectations and winning the hearts of both their customers and employees. History has proven that all lasting commerce is born from a dedication to high character, high quality, and high customer loyalty. This is why the Honest Era is a time of people over profit.

Because of their noble characteristics, companies naturally succeed. We all crave to do business with exceptional and energetic organizations that we can trust. And in return for our patronage, companies can expect to grow a more captivated and loyal following of their brand. When companies are in this era, everybody wins. The economy is strong, customers are happy, and companies are profitable.

But as history tells us, these organizations grow. And as they swell, their processes adjust, and the business changes. In

Walmart's pursuit of growth, for example, something was lost. An organization that once desired to serve people in rural communities ended up harming the small businesses around them. Everywhere a new Walmart opened, long-standing local stores were forced to permanently close their doors. In order to keep prices low, Walmart purchased more goods manufactured overseas, which meant fewer regulations on ethical working conditions. And Walton, a man who was once known to be generous, opted for hiring as few employees as possible and never paying them more than he had to.

After Walton died in 1992, customers began wising up to the retail giant's modern practices, and public hostility began to grow. By the early 2000s, Walmart became one of the most hated companies in America.[4]

As it turns out, low prices come at a high cost.

History demonstrates that as companies grow, they often begin making subtle changes and deviations to accommodate that growth. Their organizational gazes shift from honesty and quality to efficiency and quantity. They aren't Mr. Hyde yet, but they have started walking a path of transformation from noble beginnings to something they never intended to be.

2

THE EFFICIENT ERA

Addicted to More

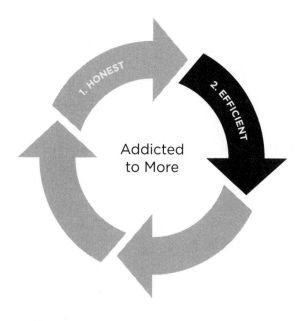

John Tyson started a chicken company from humble beginnings in 1935 out of Springdale, Arkansas. He built his business on the backbone of reliability and quality, which led to the expansion of his company into several Midwestern states. He grew the company for the next several decades, becoming vertically integrated and reaping himself not only hefty profits but also a good name in the industry.

In 1967, the company propelled toward vast expansion by focusing on increasing productivity and efficiency to meet the increasing needs of a chicken-hungry country. The company bought up competitors, expanded into the beef and pork markets, and secured lucrative contracts to supply low-cost (and coincidentally, low-nutrition) chicken nuggets to fast-food chains, such as McDonald's.

Furthermore, to meet the demand of the company's rapid growth, Tyson adopted and even pioneered some of today's controversial efficient factory farming systems. The company began engaging in practices such as loading up chickens with antibiotics and growth hormones to pack chicks closer, get them fatter faster, and get them to the public sooner.

They implemented light-changing systems to speed up the natural molting process. They moved livestock from the field to confined spaces to increase herding efficiency, and even began changing slaughter practices to reduce time. During these changes, Tyson radically shifted as an organization. The company website's history page illustrates this, titling the 1960s "Our People Are the Heart of Our Company" and the 1970s "Convenient Chicken for Everybody."[1]

Years later, they became a Fortune 500 company, making one word synonymous with poultry: *Tyson*.

But Tyson Foods' addiction to more—more chicken, more consumers, more profit—had radically altered the humble vision of their founder.

Yet, it's easy to forgive John Tyson for some of the compromises he made. He lived in a time before we fully understood the consequences of many of his decisions. Pure intentions of growth were at work.

THE GATEWAY TO DECLINE

A love for efficiency comes honestly to most people, having been implanted by their parents at a young age. We're told to use our time well, and we're cautioned against loitering or procrastination. We're not supposed to leave the lights on unless the room is in use. To do anything else would be a waste of energy and money. Ah, money. Something else we're taught to be efficient with.

As Pat Lencioni comments, "While it's difficult to argue with a parent's or teacher's or coach's motivation for instilling efficiency principles in the youngsters they're responsible for, there comes a time in life—especially in certain situations—when those very traits become problematic."[2]

He's right.

The ideas planted in us in childhood are gestated in the workplace and can be birthed as an unquenchable desire for the quick, cheap, and efficient. We brainstorm ways to lower our bottom line and increase revenue, which often include streamlining systems, purchasing cheaper raw materials, laying off those we deem unnecessary, and making sure that the remaining employees are prodded toward ever higher productivity.

All good companies must have some level of efficiency, which can be a tool to help achieve noble goals. But problems arise when efficiency becomes the goal—when it is no longer a means to an end but the end in itself.

As a result of their addiction to more, for example, Tyson's organization was soon battling worker unions on issues surrounding its treatment of employees by the end of the twentieth century. By contracting chicken suppliers, Tyson farmers were able to retain some level of freedom. But suppliers were paid low wages for their birds. In 2001, Tyson was sued for allegedly smuggling undocumented employees into America to work for low wages in poultry processing plants.[3]

Tyson has also become a target for green groups, who allege that the company has turned a blind eye to poor safety and environmental practices in their pursuit of more.

Their systems of efficiency have now caused them to be the center of blame for animal abuse on multiple occasions, with viral videos of animals shocked with cattle prods and

Chicken produced in the U.S. per year (in metric tons)

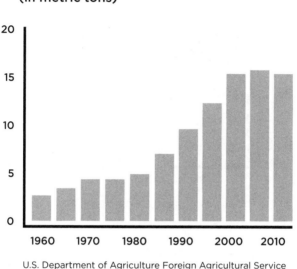

U.S. Department of Agriculture Foreign Agricultural Service

crammed into tight spaces. In 2011, for example, the Humane Society of the United States revealed that a pork farm connected to the organization was abusing piglets, even using the small animals like soccer balls.[4] Tyson initially claimed "no connection" to the farm but later backtracked in a press statement.

The food industry is a prime example, and it's much bigger than poultry farming. Centuries ago, around 80 percent of people worked the land in order to provide the food for the 100 percent. But as farming moved from a collection of family businesses to big corporations, we invented new technology that required less labor to produce greater yield. We were catapulted to our current situation: approximately

Farming food over time

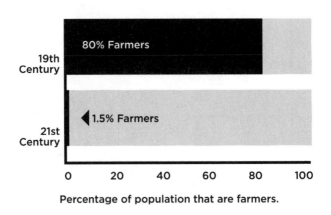

19th Century: 80% Farmers
21st Century: 1.5% Farmers

0   20   40   60   80   100

Percentage of population that are farmers.

1.5 percent of the total population grows food for the 100 percent today.[5]

In order to achieve this level of efficiency, compromises had to be made. New chemicals had to be developed to manufacture crops. Food was genetically modified to feed more with fewer units. Antibiotics were utilized so that more animals could be contained in smaller spaces without getting sick. Growth enhancers were added to feed to yield bigger animals in less time.

I don't mean to pick on the food industry. Consider a younger, sleeker organization with a more positive public image: Google. The giant was founded in 1998 with a commitment to excellence, innovation, creativity, and a clear vision for how to change the world one search phrase at a time. They valued their customers' experiences, ridding their home page of the noisy advertisements competitors were adding in droves.

The external focus on quality was also reflected inward as Google pioneered employee perks that led *Forbes* to name the company one of the best places to work. One of Google's most famed and replicated perks is their "20 percent time," which allowed employees to spend one day per week working on projects that aren't necessarily in their job descriptions. The policy became a driver of innovation, effectively spawning both Gmail and AdSense. You can practically feel the energy pulsing from an organization in the Honest Era, can't you?

THIS IS AN ERA OF PEOPLE *AND* PROFIT, WHERE COMPANIES ARE TRYING TO VALUE BOTH, EVEN THOUGH ONE SIDE ALWAYS ENDS UP LOSING.

But in recent years, Google has grown more corporate and has felt pressure from competitors, such as Apple, to increase efficiency and output. So what did the higher-ups decide? You guessed it. Bye-bye, 20 percent time.[6] It may seem like an inconsequential decision, but I think it is critical. I predict Google will either bring the policy back or hemorrhage good people and experience a decrease in innovation, which made them an industry leader in the first place.

Although organizations such as Google or Tyson are responsible for compromises they make in the pursuit of more, we can't place all the blame on their shoulders. The Efficient Era is often driven by consumers thirsty for breakneck

convenience at an ever-cheaper price. As we've seen, organizational compromises often result from giving customers
what they want.

This is an era of people *and* profit, where companies are
trying to value both, even though one side always ends up
losing. From the outside, however, few may suspect anything
is dysfunctional. If one looks only to sales reports to evaluate success, you might even assume the company is healthier
than it has ever been. Companies are increasingly proficient,
running well overall, and expanding on most every front.
Customers are content, even happy, with the increased number and lower cost of goods and services at their fingertips.
At this point, no one realizes how unsustainable the system
might be.

History teaches us that the relentless pursuit of efficiency and
expansion can lead to financial success, but it often results in
an organization that can't tell the difference between bigger
and better.

As Jim Collins, author of *How the Mighty Fall: And Why
Some Companies Never Give In*, writes:

> Launching headlong into activities that do not fit with
> your economic or resource engine is undisciplined.
> Addiction to scale is undisciplined. To neglect your core
> business while you leap after exciting new adventures is
> undisciplined. To use the organization primarily as a vehi-
> cle to increase your own personal success—more wealth,
> more fame, more power—at the expense of its long-term

Just because you can, doesn't mean you should. Or just because it's smart, doesn't mean it's right.

People Over Profit

success is undisciplined. To compromise your values or lose sight of your core purpose in pursuit of growth and expansion is undisciplined.[7]

Ultimately, I believe Collins is stating that leaving the traits of the Honest Era is undisciplined. Those tempted by the addiction to more need to realize that just because you can, doesn't mean you should. Or just because it's smart, doesn't mean it's right. Rather than salivating over new growth strategies and revenue-increasing schemes, companies moving into this era need to discipline themselves and recommit to their missions.

After all, the killer of quality is not efficiency. Rather, it's the desire to do things at a pace that can be achieved only by compromising one's values and mission. The thirst for more is not evil itself, but it is often the gateway to something that is.

3

THE DECEPTIVE ERA

Destroyed by Greed

Rewind to the late 1990s. The Great Recession hasn't hit yet, and even though the signs are emerging everywhere, no one sees it coming. The American economy is booming, unemployment is low, and consumers seem satisfied enough. But trouble is brewing beneath the surface.

Greedy bankers are making unfavorable loans to people who can't afford them. Between 2002 and 2007 before the market goes bust, an estimated $3.2 trillion in loans are made to "homebuyers with bad credit and undocumented incomes."[1]

Granting these loans helped inflate home prices and created a tidal wave of foreclosures beginning in 2008. The lending companies continued to increase short-term profits, while unknowingly digging their own graves. Their lack of integrity led to famous headlines suggesting that the Great Recession began with the Great Deception.

Meanwhile, those at the top of the economic food chain were hoarding more and more wealth, rather than proportionately investing profits into development or those who worked under them. In 1965, CEOs at America's largest companies earned about 20:1 what their average workers did. The ratio climbed to approximately 59:1 by 1989 and 199:1 by 1994. At the turn of the twenty-first century, these CEOs were earning more than their average workers at an approximate ratio of 411:1.[2]

But the Deceptive Era is not only a period of our economic history; it's also a season many companies enter. Their addiction to efficiency has driven them toward unsustainable goals and forces their focus exclusively on institutional survival. Deceptive tactics such as misleading advertising, disproportionate salaries, unsustainable workloads, and a lack of corporate accountability help form the first rainclouds of a developing storm of destruction.

CEO Salary Compared to Average Employee

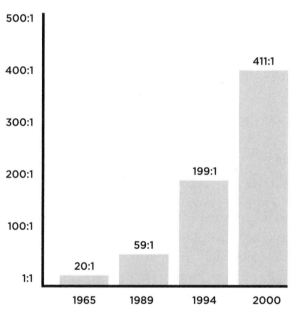

In order to sustain these trends, companies have to make additional compromises to quality and character: In the 1990s, companies shifted labor overseas with increasing frequency, opening the door to an epidemic of child labor and low-wage manufacturing. Personalized customer service gave way to automated menus and international call centers where operators wrestled to overcome language barriers when assisting customers. Fine print and false advertising became standard fare for marketing collateral.

The American automobile industry failed to produce products on par with foreign brands. Pharmaceutical companies played fast and loose with research and development, rushing drugs to market before they were ready. Agricultural companies genetically modified food and increased production with chemicals that could harm consumers.

With this perfect storm swirling throughout the marketplace, is it any wonder that America experienced one of the largest economic recessions in its history?

KNOCKING ON DEATH'S DOOR

We know that companies don't start out bad, and we know that once a company grows, it often begins making compromises to its values and vision in the name of more. But what happens when those compromises reach critical mass? What happens when profit becomes more important than the people a company serves and those who work for it? What happens when quarterly reports stand as the ultimate metric of a company's success?

The Deceptive Era is a period in the life of an institution when its mission and vision become little more than a footnote in its history. A time when founding values are preached but not practiced, and turning a buck goes from healthy to harmful. The bottom line becomes the point on the horizon where the company focuses its gaze, and anyone who gets in the way is expendable. This is an era of lies. This is an era of distortion. This is an era of profit over people.

Blinded by their short-lived financial success, organizations begin to flail by almost every other marker. A widespread denial of reality begins to creep into the culture. Low company morale is reasoned away, information is censored or spun, and higher-ups rebut naysayers. Publicity departments during this period amplify the positive, explain away the negative, and ignore anything that counters the narrative they want the public to believe.[3]

Once-loyal consumers begin to wise up in the Deceptive Era. They grow dissatisfied with lower quality, higher prices, and a creeping sense that they can no longer trust the organization. Though they often still patronize these companies—at least until new options emerge—a quiet worry metastasizes in the marketplace. The need to change is no longer knocking; it's kicking down the door.

DECEPTION BREEDS RECESSION

History demonstrates that when companies enter the Deceptive Era en masse, it always leads to recession. America has weathered twenty-eight recessions—quantified as two consecutive down quarters of GDP with a 1.5 percent rise in unemployment—from 1880 to 2010. Some lasted months, while others stretched on for years. But how many of these were self-inflicted and not caused by uncontrollable global variables?

I did some research on this question not long ago, combing through data to isolate specific patterns of US capitalism and its sole effects on causing economic recessions. The goal was to examine recessions that were generated by decisions, markets, and trends of the people in the United States. In addition, we wanted to compare these variables with consumer trust data both before and after a recession. I studied heaps of vintage advertising, company communication, business articles, books, YouTube videos, documentaries, white papers, and psychographic surveys and interviewed individuals to get a sense of the relationship between consumerism and capitalism in these specific eras of time.

At the end, I concluded there were three self-inflicted recessions during this period in US history. All were caused by a critical mass of companies operating with Deceptive Era traits.

The Panic of 1893

This recession lasted a year and five months with unemployment peaking at 18.4 percent.[4] What caused it? Years of overextension by railroad companies and the slowing of general economic expansion across the country. Debt and reckless management forced the Philadelphia and Reading Railroad into bankruptcy, which finally triggered recession, leading to a run on the banks and economic panic. More than fifteen thousand businesses failed and five hundred banks closed.[5]

Those who cannot remember the past are condemned to repeat it.

George Santayana

The Great Depression

This recession lasted three years and seven months begin-ning in 1929 with unemployment peaking at 24.9 percent.[6] What caused it? A period of rampant speculation in the 1920s culminated in a market crash of epic proportions. Over the course of two days, beginning with the infamous Black Tuesday, the stock market lost more than a quarter of its value. Uninsured bank deposits left ordinary people vul-nerable when financial institutions went belly up. American economic production dropped by 50 percent, the economies of nearly every developed country were affected, and the rip-pling effects spanned more than a decade.

The Great Recession

This recession lasted one year and six months beginning in 2008 with unemployment peaking at 10.2 percent.[7] As mentioned above, it was caused by risky lending practices, a massive credit bubble, and unethical business practices throughout the marketplace. The effects of this period are still being felt as I write.

Name	Year	Duration	Unemployment Rate
The Panic of 1893	1893	1 yr. 5 mos.	18.4%
The Great Depression	1929	3 yrs. 7 mos.	24.9%
The Great Recession	2008	1 yr. 6 mos.	10.2%

These three recessions are starkly similar. All begin with an era of impressive economic growth and high consumer trust. But in each case, trust begins to decline two to five years prior to disaster. You can almost feel the economic fabric unraveling. After recession, trust plummets when the masses become acutely aware of which companies value profit over people. The public wises up to greed, unethical processes, and dishonest advertisements.

But consumer trust doesn't fall into a black hole or give way to eternal cynicism. It reemerges as the public establishes new loyalties with companies that embody honesty, quality, and integrity. With a slew of Honest Era start-ups arriving on the scene, mature brands that once owned consumer loyalty are forced to deploy major trust-building campaigns to compete.

You don't need to rewind to the late 1990s to learn about the Deceptive Era. You could visit the 1920s or 1890s, or really any time in any company's life when greed is king. Regardless of when they enter the Deceptive Era, these companies will face a choice: change or die.

4

THE APOLOGETIC ERA

A Revolutionary Act

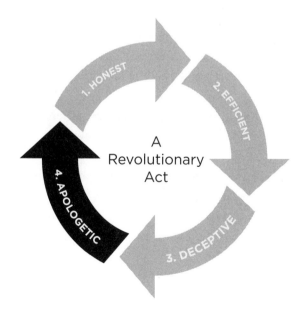

Nobody likes a lousy pizza.

Few things force a person to shout expletives faster than blotting a greasy pie with a paper towel or chewing on rubbery crust like a field-bound cow. And yet, this is exactly the experience that Domino's Pizza customers reported having in the early 2000s. "The sauce tastes like ketchup," one taste tester remarked. Another gave feedback Domino's admits hearing frequently: "Domino's pizza crust to me is like cardboard."[1]

The pizza chain and its flagship product hadn't always underwhelmed customers. It was founded by two brothers in the 1960s with a commitment to high-quality pies and "fast, free delivery." By 1985, Domino's was the fastest-growing pizza company in America, with stores opening around the world.[2] But in their rigorous pursuit of expansion—opening the fifteen hundredth store outside the United States in 1997, "including seven stores in one day on five continents simultaneously"—something had been lost.[3]

Their pizza's low quality was infamous among consumers, and their customer service wasn't wowing anyone. By 2009, Domino's stock had dipped dangerously low on the New York Stock Exchange, and something had to be done to combat negative brand equity. Executives were faced with a daunting decision to either continue their current course or reinvent the way they did business. They mustered the courage to choose the latter.

"There was a day we woke up and we realized we just couldn't go any further unless we fixed the pizza," one higher-up remarked.[4]

Domino's worked to reinvent their core recipe, combing through fifty different spice combinations and fifteen sauces. They tested "dozens" of cheese blends—with actual cheese rather than the oil derivatives they'd been using. They opted for honesty in a national media campaign that admitted poor pizza quality, apologizing to customers and announcing their efforts to improve.[5]

The pizza giant even promised a greater level of transparency, which included a "pledge to show actual products in advertising rather than enhanced versions lovingly tended to by professional food artists."[6] A website was launched where customers could post real photos to be used in marketing materials.

By admitting their errors and restoring a corporate commitment to honesty, transparency, quality, and customer service, Domino's pizza began to recover. By 2014, stock prices were soaring to new heights.

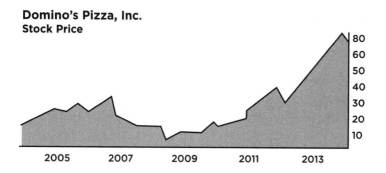

Domino's Pizza, Inc.
Stock Price

Upon announcing the new initiative, an executive at the pizza chain remarked, "This is new. It's different. It's a new Domino's. It's a new era."[7]

The executive didn't know how right she was. A company that began with honesty, grew addicted to more, and opted for deception had unwittingly entered a new epoch in corporate history.

Welcome to the Apologetic Era, Domino's. You're not alone.

BECOMING WHO YOU ONCE WERE

When deception lays hold of an organization, an invisible clock begins ticking down. Consumers get fed up and eventually reach their tipping point. They finally begin to jump ship and offer their business to more noble organizations. At that moment, decision makers must decide if they will apologize for their missteps and recommit to their founding standards. Some don't, which usually leads to bankruptcy. But many do because they know that a grueling commitment to better business is the only way to regain consumer trust . . . and survive.

Think about a situation where a married man or woman gets caught cheating on his or her spouse. If there's any hope of restoration, the offending party must apologize and begin living above reproach through increased accountability and openness. There is no hope otherwise. So it is in the relationship between companies and the consumers they've deceived and betrayed. If they do not rectify the relationship—and quickly—the marketplace marriage will end.

The Apologetic Era is about restoring. Restoring confidence. Restoring trust. Restoring health. Restoring faith. Restoring hope, mission, quality, and accountability. It's about restoring transparency and compassion.

During this period a company is apologetic, rectifying, and reenergized. They are righting wrongs and improving from the inside out. They replace defective leaders with those who are constitutionally incapable of compromising the company's moral fabric. Employee morale increases as people regain hope that they are giving their time and efforts to an organization that cares.

Consumers remain cautious, having been burned too many times, but they are also eager and receptive to honest admissions of guilt and tangible efforts to improve. There's something gratifying about hearing, "I'm sorry." Consumers are homesick for a company that cares, and an apology can help heal hurts if done well.

Other than Domino's, we might look to General Motors for an example of how this era functions. In 2008, company executives began owning up to their failures. They admitted they had "disappointed," "betrayed," and violated the trust of customers.[8] Among the list of confessions were producing vehicles "below industry standards," too many brands and dealers, a bias toward gas-guzzling trucks and SUVs, and "lackluster" designs.

Alongside their public statement, General Motors released a powerful commercial, with voiceovers dripping with apologetic candor that admitted mistakes:

> Let's be completely honest. No company wants to go through this. But we're not witnessing the death of the American car. We're witnessing the rebirth of the American car. General Motors needs to start over in order to get stronger. There was a time when eight different brands made sense. Not anymore. There was a time when our cost structure could compete worldwide. Not anymore. Reinvention is the only way we can fix this. And fix it, we will.[9]

Toyota released a similar ad in 2010 after their pursuit of efficiency allowed the release of cars with a dangerous brake malfunction: "In recent days, our company hasn't been living up to the standards that you've come to expect from us or that we expect from ourselves. That's why 172,000 Toyota and dealership employees are dedicated to make things right." Toyota stopped production in order to repair the mistakes so as to "restore your faith in our company."[10]

American Airlines is another, though admittedly less stark, example. Like many of their competitors, American had struggled to provide a quality flying experience and satisfactory customer service until recently, when a merger provided an opportunity to chart a new path. They reevaluated their processes and procedures before releasing a renovated fleet of birds. American refined menu options, increased seat comfortability and legroom, added Wi-Fi to nearly all aircraft, and added in-seat entertainment systems on all new planes.

The company promised to become "a new American," stating, "We've changed our look on the outside to reflect the progress we've made on the inside."[11] Will these companies fully enter the Apologetic Era? Will they shift the weight of their focus back from profits to people? Only time will tell. Regardless, they demonstrate a trend in corporate life cycles where a company begins to turn the ship back toward the Honest Era. Their efforts don't guarantee they'll be on top again, or even in the game. It just means they're giving themselves a fighting chance.

As Jim Collins has noted, "The signature of the truly great is not the absence of difficulty but the ability to recover from setbacks. Great companies can fall and recover if they are willing to make difficult decisions to do difficult things in difficult times."[12]

But now I must make a confession. Though you may not have been aware, an elephant stood in the room as we explored the cycle of capitalistic behavior: companies don't have to operate in this system. Established organizations can move back into the Honest Era and remain there. And new companies can start out there and never depart.

As the founder of an organization that's not that old, I'm at a place where we're still operating in the Honest Era. I can see the temptations to move forward and get swept up in the cycle. That as we'd grow, we'd compromise our values.

So I decided to find out how Sevenly—and other organizations like ours—could avoid this. Could we escape the tractor-beam pull that had drawn in so many others? I didn't know, but I was determined to find out. Along the way, I discovered how to break the system and live with purpose while being even more successful.

PART 2

WITH UNDERSTANDING COMES CHANGE

Whole Foods. REI. Chick-fil-A. Patagonia. In-N-Out Burger.

What do these brands have in common? Each have managed to remain in the Honest Era—or at least have never fallen into the Deceptive Era—despite a long history.

A few years ago, I decided to study companies like these to analyze what made them successful. I recorded human resource practices, ethics and responsibility standards, marketing language, and customer loyalty levels. Then one night, I opened Lyn Richards' *Handling Qualitative Data*. (Yes, I'm a nerd like that.) Her process of research aims to gather an in-depth understanding of not only human behavior but also the motivations governing such behavior. It investigates the *why* and *how*, not just *what, where,* and *when.*

So I returned to the organizations I'd been surveying and dug deeper. What motivated them to remain ruthlessly committed to their vision and seemingly impervious to compromise? Which beliefs drove them to do business the way they did?

After studying dozens of leaders and organizations who had broken the system, I discovered seven core beliefs shared by almost all of them:

- People Matter

- Truth Wins

- Transparency Frees

- Authenticity Attracts

- Quality Speaks

- Generosity Returns

- Courage Sustains

Most of the companies I studied would be befuddled by these phrases. They don't appear in their company handbooks and aren't engraved in brass at the door of their headquarter offices. But the ideas were present, animating everything from their marketing materials to employee appreciation to customer service commitments. The perfect company is a myth. No organization—particularly a large one—acts with integrity at all times. But together these beliefs form the rudder that can keep even the largest corporate barge on course.

At first blush, these beliefs didn't sound innovative. They were simple. Almost too simple. They were more reminiscent of the values parents teach children than a cutting-edge corporate sketch in the *Harvard Business Review*. But as I've pondered it, I've come to see that humans have struggled with these virtues since the beginning of time. To not lie, to not manipulate or deceive, and to not mistreat those who have treated you poorly. However, I think the simplicity of these concepts is also the secret to their power. Almost as simple as Moses' Ten Commandments, these beliefs are common human morals, and even the most hardheaded employee or consumer can grasp them. And they have formed the cornerstones of some of the most successful leaders and organizations in marketplace history.

And yet, these time-tested philosophies are countercultural and counterintuitive. They often rub against basic business tendencies like sandpaper. Upon further inspection, these beliefs are as revolutionary as they are simplistic. Though these beliefs are rooted in old wisdom, they can empower you to forge new frontiers in the marketplace and in life. Even beyond business, these beliefs are proven principles to living with purpose, generating greater success, and creating the world we all crave.

If you can't explain it to a six-year-old, you don't understand it yourself.

___

Albert Einstein

5

PEOPLE MATTER

One of the most difficult and yet important things a team can do when launching a company is craft a tagline. Though only a handful of words, it will become your banner, your rallying cry, your flag in the sand. A tagline shapes customers' first impressions of who you are and why you exist. The Sevenly launch team knew how crucial this task was when we started in 2011, so we deliberated for weeks before settling on a short, bold declaration: "Do good."

The phrase seemed to express what our organization set out to accomplish, and it resonated with our earliest customers. Over several months, we wove this phrase into the fabric of our operations. We posted it on our website, printed it on business cards, featured it in our videos, and stamped it on the labels of the shirts we sold.

Little did we know, the first Sevenly tagline was not long for this world.

A year later, I met a friend who runs an organization in the same industry for lunch near the Sevenly headquarters in Costa Mesa, California. We chatted casually about our companies and current projects while chowing down on some spicy Mexican grub at Taco Asylum. The next day, he e-mailed me to say that he thought our tagline created marketplace confusion with his organization. I didn't agree with his assessment, but the possibility of a legal battle forced me to ask, "Is this tagline worth fighting for?" The answer was no.

Our team went back to the drawing board, this time asking more profound questions than before. We began to explore the Sevenly "whyology":

- Why did we start this company?

- Why are we passionate about our mission?

- Why do we give away money to charities rather than keeping it for ourselves?

Each question pushed us back to a common answer: because we believe that people matter. Our business was like a complex system of roads, but every path originated from the

How you make others feel about themselves says a lot about you.

——

People Over Profit

#PeopleOverProfit

same source: a conviction about the value of the individuals who made our company possible.

As it turns out, "Do good" was a weak tagline. It answered only the *what* and not the *why* of our organization. Additionally, "Do good" is easy, but "People matter" is difficult. It not only clarified our mission but also forced us to reevaluate every facet of the way we operated.

When I researched companies that were breaking the destructive cycle of organizational behavior later on, I discovered that they, too, were animated by this belief. Like Jed Clampett's black gold discovery, our team had unwittingly stumbled across a cornerstone belief shared by all companies that strive to remain in the Honest Era.

MADE OF PEOPLE, NOT PARTS

The greatest hurdle to becoming a "people-matter" organization is sight. The marketplace, left to itself, doesn't see people. It sees pieces to a puzzle. It sees potential purchasers. It sees zeros and dollar signs and credit-card swipes and bottom lines. The marketplace does not naturally differentiate between a customer who is loyal and one who is disloyal; it sees only if they purchase goods. The marketplace does not notice whether an employee working in a warehouse is treated well or degraded; it sees only if they are productive.

It takes work, therefore, for a company to do business with eyes wide open. Organizations that operate under this belief take account of how every person they touch is treated and then implement high standards. When you say a company believes that people matter, it means they hold to the following convictions:

- People are valuable.

- No person is worth more than another.

- Every person deserves to be treated fairly and with respect.

- Organizations should be empathetic to all people they touch.

A company is made of people. It is nothing if there are no people. Devaluing people who compose a company is like a government disregarding its citizens. It can work, but only for a time. For this reason, "people-matter" organizations focus on three kinds of stakeholders.

1. Team Members

If employee morale falls, the company is not far behind. Are those who work with you tired and overworked or excited and stimulated? Are they undercompensated or financially validated? Are they encouraged to think differently and dream big or check off a task list and punch a clock? Are they in the loop about the direction the organization is moving or kept on a need-to-know basis? Do they feel like cogs in a machine or integral partners in pursuit of a greater mission?

The answer to these questions will reveal whether or not a company believes their team members matter.

Companies who live by this belief maintain a high level of communication with every layer of their teams. They encourage employees to be themselves and work within their natural talents and passions. Team members are provided ways to develop and grow and advance, and don't feel weighed down with complex or meaningless rules and policies. Those who work for "people-matter" organizations are often proud of it. They wear clothes or carry coffee mugs with their company logo, and they brag to their friends about where they work. If team members matter, team members *know* they matter.

Do you want to see a company that values its employees? Look no further than Clif Bar, maker of tasty treats made with high-quality natural ingredients. Founded in 1992, the company now has three hundred employees who rave about where they work. A few years ago, Clif Bar moved to a new set of digs complete with four wide-open gardens, a fleet of loaner bikes available for running errands, and a fitness center with a climbing wall, yoga room, two massage rooms, and free access to five personal trainers and nutritionists. Employees get 2.5 hours of paid gym time per week.

Clif Bar's perks don't stop there. Every employee gets a $350 stipend for entering races and competitions and $1,000 per year for eco-conscious home improvements. Each week, there is a company-wide breakfast with free food where a Clif Bar fan letter is read. They can choose from several flexible work options to fit their unique schedules, and after seven years of service, they are given a six- to eight-week sabbatical. Oh, and if you love your golden retriever, don't worry. The office is dog friendly too.[1]

Do you think the Clif Bar team members know they matter?

Exactly.

2. Customers

If there is no one willing to pay for what you're producing, you might as well start sending out résumés. Customers pay our salaries. It's that simple. Yet too many companies treat their customers like a mere metric of profitability. If patrons aren't happy, they may let them walk, rather than work to meet their needs or rectify failures. Somewhere along the line they've begun operating as though customers exist to serve them rather than the other way around.

By contrast, a "people-matter" organization works to make customers feel special and valued. They don't just tell patrons that they want their business; they work to retain it. Companies that operate by this belief don't have just good eyes to see people; they have attentive ears as well. When customers complain, it is taken seriously and addressed with empathy and compassion. And when customers are happy, steps are taken to keep it that way. While cutting corners might increase profits, these businesses refuse to do anything that would shortchange customers and erode trust. In fact, they go above and beyond to remind their customers how much they are appreciated and valued.

When you think of quality customer service, airlines don't usually come to mind. But Southwest has continued to be an innovator in this industry. They are known for low-cost fares and flight crews that work hard to make trips enjoyable or even comedic. Additionally, they are one of the few airlines that has refused to charge customers for checking a bag or penalize them with change fees if they need to reschedule.

Southwest's commitment to valuing people over profit was on display recently when they worked to accommodate a traveler en route from Los Angeles to Denver. The man was flying to Colorado to see his three-year-old grandson for the last time. The boy had been beaten into a coma by his mother's boyfriend and was being taken off life support that evening. The customer's wife called Southwest to book a last-minute fare, explaining the difficult situation. But Los Angeles traffic and the security lines at LAX being what they are, the man did not arrive at the gate until twelve minutes after the plane was scheduled to take off. When he arrived, he was stunned to find the pilot waiting for him.

"They can't go anywhere without me, and I wasn't going anywhere without you," the pilot said. "Now relax. We'll get you there. And again, I'm so sorry."[2]

This pilot understood that people matter. He didn't see the man as just a passenger, but as a person. A fellow human made of flesh, emotions, and a hurting heart.

Trader Joe's grocery chain provides another example of

a company that believes customers matter. Recently, an 89-year-old World War II veteran was snowed in without much food in his pantry. His daughter phoned around to several grocers inquiring about delivery services. Trader Joe's was the only one that said they did. Turns out, they actually don't but they were willing to help out the elderly man. When the groceries arrived, the man was not charged for a delivery fee . . . *or* for the groceries.[3]

Had the manager of this Trader Joe's location thought only of profitability, he would have dismissed the request and gotten back to work selling soup cans. But because he recognized that his business exists to serve, assist, and benefit people, he had permission to say yes.

These are more than heartwarming stories; they are tales that illustrate different kinds of companies—those that allowed employees to break protocol and bend rules in order to serve customers well. The pilot chose people over profit, and so did the manager of the grocery store, and they did so because they knew their organization valued customers as much as they did.

3. Vendors

Businesses are most likely to pay attention to the needs and wants of customers and employees because they are closely connected to the organization itself. But vendors—those who provide goods and services that allow a company to operate—are often overlooked. Yet these stakeholders are critical.

It's easier to mistreat those in developing nations where much of our manufacturing takes place due to the lack of effective regulations and employees' work conditions. Evils like child labor, poverty-level wages, and inhumane shifts create barbaric workplaces. In recent years, however, many companies have become more aware of the practices of those throughout their supply chain. Organizations that believe people matter are demanding fair treatment of those who contribute to the products they sell and services they provide.

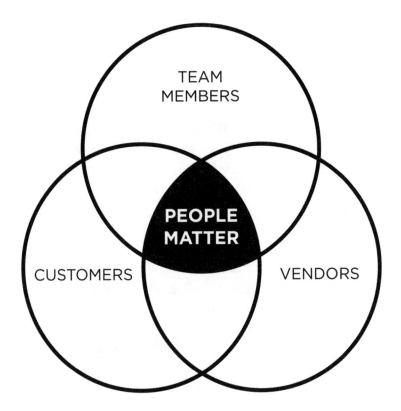

Apolis Global is a great example as a socially motivated fashion company based out of Los Angeles. They've worked hard to become a "Certified B Corporation," which means they exceed social and environmental standards while remaining transparent and accountable. They employ artisans in various nations to bridge economic development and commerce.

More than seventy-three craftsman working in both Israel and Palestine manufacture leather sandals. The business partnership with Apolis has opened up communication channels between Tel-Aviv and Hebron, helping to dismantle misconceptions between the two people groups. In Bangladesh, more than twenty-one Apolis artisans have manufactured over forty thousand bags. Apolis' work has provided jobs as well as literacy, nutrition, and finance classes. In Uganda, Apolis employs twelve cotton farmers to produce fabric for a custom-made briefcase. More than a thousand units have been sold so far, and their investment in the cotton crop is helping to rejuvenate a once-strong industry in the region.[4]

Apolis is a small but growing company that is demonstrating how to value vendors as well as customers and employees.

Companies are good at valuing some of the people they touch, but few value all of them. For example, an organization may pay their employees well and offer great benefits, but they become inwardly focused, entitled, and provide a low level of customer service. Or a company may realize that they must value customers, so they offer them great service and low-priced products. But in order to achieve this, they overlook the low wages and poor work conditions of overseas manufacturers.

Organizations can't just look out for executives. Or board members. Or shareholders. Or high-dollar customers. A person who is purchasing goods and services from a company is as important as those who are selling them or brainstorming new ones from a corporate conference room. The customer in Wichita, Kansas, must be valued alongside the marketing executive in Midtown Manhattan, the warehouse worker in Fort Wayne, Indiana, the sales clerk in Phoenix, Arizona, and the manufacturers in Kunshan, China.

Companies that believe people matter must believe that *all* people matter.

AN UNSTOPPABLE ENTERPRISE

In the Deceptive and Efficient Eras, people are valuable only so long as they are profitable. But companies in the Honest Era recognize that individuals are intrinsically and equally valuable. They all have struggles, excitements, and joys, and no one should be forced to sacrifice their dignity or humanity for the sake of profitability.

At Sevenly, I knew that it wouldn't be too difficult to raise money for a worthy cause. But it would take resolve to ensure that people were valued in every nook and cranny of our organization. So we took drastic steps to protect the belief that everyone is worth loving, caring for, and serving well.

We hired a full-time staff person—a director of culture and community—tasked with making sure our employees are happy, valued, and building strong relationships with one another. We make sure that even in our office, we are valuing people over profit. And this person holds us accountable. Don't fool yourself into thinking that being radically people-centric can happen by osmosis. This must be built in.

We have learned that what drives people more than anything is purpose. Not pay and benefits, but purpose. So we work hard to connect the Sevenly team members with the things they truly desire. We let them partake in storytelling, and connect every element of their job to communicate our causes back to consumers. Whether it is the art process or the videos we make or the choosing of the charities, we want our team invested. And we make sure they know their opinions count.

Even when we need to let someone go, we do it differently. We look at employment as a season. Everybody, including me, will transition into this company for a season and transition out at some point. No one will be here forever. Termination doesn't mean they are a bad person or are worthless. It just means that they may not work well here at this current moment. It's just as unfair for the employee as it is for us to keep them in their current position when we know it doesn't work.

Yet even if you believe all these things to be true, termination can still be a devastating process. So at Sevenly, we have a unique twist on the golden rule: fire others the way you

FIRE OTHERS THE WAY YOU WOULD WANT TO BE FIRED.

———————

would want to be fired. When we explain our reasoning, we never discuss personal flaws; we always talk about the work. We try to provide them with a generous severance regardless of their tenure, and don't penny pinch. Why? Because we know they are people with spouses and kids and houses.

We've let outgoing employees keep their computers, and even have extended their benefits. If at all possible, we write them a letter of recommendation extolling their positive traits. When they leave, we offer them an opportunity to come back to the office to celebrate them with the team. We have the team go around and affirm them by sharing what they love about them and we even pray over them. People who transition out are not fired employees; we consider them alumni.

Our goal is that when a former team member leaves our company they'll say, "It didn't work out for me at Sevenly in the end, but they are a darn good company."

We also attempt to value our customers and vendors. Our goal is to give every customer who writes us on Facebook or social media a response from an actual team member. We don't have automated messages, but rather treat people like people. (Novel idea, I know.) There is even a phone number on our website that doesn't get rerouted to another country. Call it, and we'll answer. And if for some reason we don't, we'll get right back to you.

All of our printed apparel is made with cotton that is woven in Los Angeles. It's not the cheapest, but it affirms those who live at our back door. Those who cut and sew the garment or print on the garment are our friends. I've walked the facilities, met the manufacturers, and verified that garments are made with the utmost ethical care. We refuse to support a faceless manufacturer, even if it would save us money.

We often forget that every organization is just a group of people—individuals with hearts, minds, desires, hopes, and feelings who are enlivened by a common mission. When we realize that the power of our success comes solely from the thing our companies are made of, we can begin to change our world. By adopting "people-matter" principles and fusing them into an organization, companies can build a loyal tribe of individuals who will fight alongside their leaders and help build an unstoppable enterprise.

6

TRUTH WINS

This Thanksgiving seemed like most others. Morgan sat on a couch in a turkey coma watching television while the rest of his family slouched in other parts of the house. Then a news story caught his attention. The reporter told of two over-weight teenagers in New York who were suing McDonald's, blaming the restaurant chain for their conditions.

That's when Morgan Spurlock had the idea to make a documentary to expose the truth about the nutritional value of McDonald's menu.

Spurlock ate three McDonald's meals a day for an entire month, never rejecting an offer to supersize and never consuming anything that wasn't on the fast-food chain's menu.

He also had to eat every item at least once. Burgers, fish fillets, and ice cream sundaes dripping with Strawberry-flavored goo. Handfuls of greasy french fries wiped with corn-syrup–laden ketchup and slice upon slice of processed cheese.

What effect did this diet have on his body? In less than three weeks, Spurlock had experienced weight gain, skyrocketing cholesterol, depression, liver erosion, and twitching outbreaks. By the end, he developed a dependency on the food strangely reminiscent of a drug addict.

"My cholesterol shot up 65 points. My liver basically turned to fat. It was so filled with fat the doctors said it was like pâté; it was reaching a toxic level, putting me in risk of having non-alcoholics type of hepatitis, hardening of the liver, cirrhosis of the liver. It got really frightening for a while," Spurlock said. "And the impact it had on my sex life was also another aspect my girlfriend didn't anticipate."[1]

When the *Supersize Me* documentary released in 2004, audiences flocked in droves. Not because the hypothesis was particularly shocking—most people assume McDonald's food is bad for you—but because someone was willing to tell the truth about a company that hid behind sexy advertising and carefully crafted language rather than shooting straight with the public. Spurlock served up a healthy portion of truth, and the American public, hungry for honesty, gobbled it up with more than $11 million in ticket sales.

More than a successful documentary, *Supersize Me* was a

Rather than love, than money, than fame, give me truth.

———

Henry David Thoreau

falling domino that started a trend in films shedding light on corporate and institutional lies. In 2006, *An Inconvenient Truth* told the story of global environmental degradation of which so many were blissfully unaware. *Sicko*, in 2007, exposed the racket that is the American health care industry and called pharmaceutical companies to the carpet for their harmful practices. The year 2008 brought *Food, Inc.*, which told the truth about the food industry in a way that helped spur on a national trend in organic meat, dairy, and produce. And *Waiting for Superman*, in 2010, uncovered an education system that is failing millions. Combined ticket sales for these films exceeded $58 million.

Is it a coincidence that these films emerged in a time of widespread marketplace deception? I think not.

The documentary industry is not the only one that has thrived off the belief that truth wins. Businesses have been built on this philosophy too. Established companies have flourished on this idea for decades, and start-ups have prospered from it.

CarMax, for example, opened its first store in 1993 with a belief that they had "a better way to buy and sell used cars." By the late twentieth century, the automobile industry had become known as one of the most dishonest in existence. "Used car salesman" had turned into a parody phrase to describe someone who was not trustworthy.

The company decided to change this, launching dealerships with a no-haggle policy. The clearly marked price on the windshield was the selling price—period. Every car was put through a rigorous evaluation process to ensure it met the highest standards. If your current car passed their test, CarMax would buy it from you even if you didn't purchase another vehicle from them.

CarMax also pays their employees well, eliminating graded commission structures that can breed dishonesty. They allow customers to view financing options on screen directly from loan companies so they can select their preferred option. Pair this with award-winning customer service, and you have a recipe for success.

This innovative car company now operates more than one hundred locations across America and has sold in excess of four million automobiles. They have been named one of *Fortune*'s "100 Best Companies to Work For" every year for nearly a decade. CarMax is a powerful tale of an organization that's generating incredible success from refusing to tell lies.

Or consider another company in the same industry with a similar name: CarFax. The company was founded in the 1980s to combat odometer fraud, but later developed into a vehicle history reporting service that was delivered via fax machine (hence the name). Today, the company has obtained title information from motor vehicle departments in every state in the union and ten Canadian provinces. Additionally, they have access to more than ten billion records from more than 34,000 additional sources. Consumers are no longer unprotected when they purchase a used car. CarFax will tell them if the vehicle has been in an accident, had major repairs, or has any manufacturer recalls.

The success of these two companies operating in one of the most notoriously dishonest industries teaches the same lesson of Spurlock's fast-food feeding frenzy documentary: truth wins, especially in an era where deception has reigned for too long.

TELL IT EVEN IF IT HURTS

The world is full of lies. Actually, that is an understatement. We're bathing in lies. We buy lies. We eat lies for breakfast, lunch, and dinner. And the marketplace is the biggest lie factory around. According to a recent survey of forty thousand Americans, 93 percent of employees lie "regularly and habitually in the workplace."[2] And it takes a toll on society.

"We lie all the time, and it wears us out," says Brad Blanton, psychotherapist and author of *Radical Honesty*. "We manage our companies through a series of delusional clichés: 'The customer is always right'; 'I'm not angry'; 'We're proceeding according to plan.' But we all know better than that. Lying takes a huge toll in terms of stress, anxiety, and depression."[3]

In a world full of lies, businesses that refuse to compromise truth will capture imaginations and earn consumer trust. Organizations that live by this belief will do these three things.

Honesty is more than not lying. It is truth telling, truth speaking, truth living, and truth loving.

———

James E. Faust

• Tell the truth completely: Everyone gets the same story. Entry-level employees aren't sold a bill of goods that executives wouldn't recognize. And customers aren't fed "facts" that employees know are falsehoods. All people an organization touches receive identical information.

• Tell the truth quickly: Organizations have a tendency to withhold the truth in certain situations. If there is a systemic failure, they will often sit on an apology for days or even months. "Truth-wins" companies know that ignoring the booger on your face will only draw attention to it. They know that failure to respond quickly can erode trust at warp speed, especially in a digital age where your silence creates a space for others' words to fill. When important information becomes available, it should be disseminated quickly.

• Tell the truth clearly: Organizations often claim they've told the truth when they have shared only a partial truth. Withholding critical information creates distortions and can have the same effect as telling a lie. On the other hand, sometimes organizations tell *more* than the truth, releasing information that's spun, sensationalized, or exaggerated. Organizations that believe truth wins aim for accuracy.

A commitment to honesty begins with executives. Do you speak directly to those who work for you and with you, providing them with a complete picture of where the organization is headed and how this may affect them? Do they have the freedom to speak honestly to you without fear of stonewalling or backlash? If you don't have a culture that values honesty, you cannot build a company that deals honestly.

Like all internal commitments, a belief that truth wins will spread to external relationships with customers and competitors. For a negative example, see a recent Coca-Cola commercial where the soda company brags about helping people consume fewer calories. No, seriously. "Across our portfolio of over 650 beverages, we now offer 180 low- and no-calorie choices," the commercial's narrator says before bragging about how one can of Coca-Cola has 140 "happy" calories, which consumers can spend on "extra" activities. As the commercial concludes, the fine print notes, "Calories burned may vary." Really? Who would've guessed that?[4]

Actually, advertising and marketing are spaces where organizations are most tempted to abandon the truth or tell only part of it. The Better Business Bureau was actually formed in 1912 after an attorney for Coca-Cola stated in a courtroom, "All advertising is exaggerated. Nobody believes it."[5] In some ways, I suppose, not much has changed over the last century.

If you want to know whether a company believes that truth wins, just search their marketing and advertising for "weasel words," which are modifiers that give a false impression without being flat-out lies. The name comes from the egg-eating habits of the weasel, an animal that sucks the inside of the egg but leaves the shell intact. Similarly, weasel words are hollow claims that look and sound good to consumers but are left empty.

A company, for example, may claim their drug will "virtually" cure an illness without admitting it can reduce but not eliminate the condition. Or a food company may say the product is "fortified" or "enriched" with iron without mentioning that the mineral appears only in trace amounts. Or a beer company may claim that there is "no other drink like it." This is technically true—no one has the exact formula in the exact same can or bottle—but there are actually dozens of products that are indistinguishable.

These are the types of tactics that allow banks to collect massive overdraft charges from unsuspecting customers, retailers to suck out the value of a gift card after a balance has remained unused for a period of time, and household cleaning supply manufacturers to craft fake social media reviews to give the impression that their products are better than they actually are.

Companies that rely on these tactics internally and externally can survive for a time, but consumers are keener than they assume and will wise up eventually. That's why organizations that believe truth wins refuse to mask potentially damaging information, exaggerate, selectively curate the facts, spin, or rely on weasel words and distortions to sell their goods or services. They know that the path of dishonesty leads to a catastrophic cul-de-sac of marketplace mistrust, but the fastest road to true and lasting success is a highway called truth.

THE TRUTH IS IN THE DETAILS

I recognized that a commitment to honesty can build trust with competitors, colleagues, employees, and customers in a skeptical marketplace filled with lies when I founded Sevenly. We implanted the belief that truth wins deep into our corporate culture. We needed to be aggressive because the stakes were even higher for a company like ours.

Sevenly is in the business of cause marketing. We're not just telling the products' stories but also the peoples' stories. This can be tricky, fraught with the temptation to craft campaigns that prey on emotions or sensationalize. In our industry, truth is often less marketable than a lie or a half-truth or a truth on steroids. Even a momentary lapse in honesty for a company like Sevenly that manages charitable giving for others could be a catastrophe. A white lie from one person on our team on a minor detail could cast a shadow on our entire brand. So we are careful to protect truth on all sides—with our customers, vendors, and employees.

To guard against dishonesty, our team spends a lot of time in the discovery phase, gathering information about the charities we work with. We don't set out to craft compelling stories, but rather to find the most compelling charities and then tell their stories accurately. We choose charities for whom the truth is wild enough that we don't need to lie. While this protects us from spinning or sensationalizing, it doesn't obliterate the temptation. So we've also committed to truth in all our marketing. You'll never find asterisks or fine print or hidden fees on our website. We run away from weasel words and fuzzy language.

After a campaign concludes, we post photos and videos and results, sending them to those who contributed to that campaign. If we build a well in Brazil, and you contributed to it, you'll receive email proof of the well and pictures of the difference made in that community. This holds us accountable to always keep the promises we make to our customers.

We also opt for honesty with our vendors and selected charities. When we ask a charity to partner with us, for example, we never make promises about how much money we'll raise. We're honest that we don't know how motivated customers may be and resist the urge to overpromise.

Sevenly also takes care to be honest with its employees. We don't hire anyone until we've drafted a Position Results Description (PRD) that outlines all expectations in terms of results and performance. We want to be honest about what the person is being hired to do and what will be required of him or her. The potential employee has to agree to this before we'll make the hire. Our hope is that we'll never hear an employee say, "When I was hired, I never knew *this* would be a part of my job," or "You hired me to do something else than I'm doing."

You may be wondering if honesty is just good morals or if it can also be a springboard to success. According to Sue Unerman and Jonathan Salem Baskin, who surveyed in-depth case studies of more than fifty global brands and research conducted on hundreds of companies, the latter is true. In their book, *Tell the Truth: Honesty Is Your Most Powerful Marketing Tool*, they stated, "Brands that have a process for telling the truth are likely to sell more products, make more money, and keep more customers loyal—through any medium, in every market."[6]

Additionally, researcher Paul Whiteley of Essex University has observed that an increase in marketplace dishonesty is usually accompanied by economic downturn.[7]

Every day you have a choice to be honest or deceptive. If you commit to telling the truth, you will win. You'll win more trust, you'll win more business, and you'll win more peace of mind. You'll break the system and be even more successful.

Honesty really is the best policy after all.

7

TRANSPARENCY FREES

Buffer isn't just the annoying thing your computer does when you're trying to stream videos. It's also the name of one of the most transparent companies in America.

As a social media management tool, Buffer might be expected to operate on the leading edge of business trends. But some would say their commitment to openness borders on the obsessive. Every employee's information is public within the company—from the highest-ranking executive to the part-time clerk. No one wonders how much money another team member makes or what their equity is worth; it's all readily available.

Even employees' sleep habits are known. Everyone is issued

Honesty and transparency make you vulnerable. Be honest and transparent anyway.

—

Mother Teresa

a Jawbone UP wristband that tracks daily steps, nutrition, sleep patterns, and more. Buffer has also implemented a productivity app called iDoneThis, where team members log what they've accomplished and what they're improving on. Some recent examples of entries include, "Four day streak of getting up at 6 a.m.," "Back to 10 minutes of consistent daily meditation," and "Need to do some Pilates."[1] They can even track what self-improvement books they're reading. Since the company pays for employees to grab any Kindle book they want, employees are posting titles often.

Buffer cofounder Leo Widrich says that committing to transparency company-wide is one of the best business decisions he's ever made. Public salaries allowed them to establish a formula for determining pay that makes hiring a lot easier. It reduces some of the contempt among coworkers that is common in workplaces. And publicizing personal productivity has created an environment of encouragement and support among team members.[2]

This small tech company has developed an open culture because they believe it is good for business. But it also has placed them smack dab in the middle of a transparency trend that is sweeping the American marketplace. An increasing number of companies today are bending over backward to be more forthcoming with everyone their business touches. For example:

- The shoe company Timberland has been working to improve factory conditions. They set up a website where customers can map their progress.[3]

- Jason Goldberg of Fab shares his company's financials, but also divulges his personal vacation plans.

- The entrepreneur empowerment organization goBRANDgo! posts all of its financials—revenue, cash account balances, credit card balances, lines of credit, and more—on a wall of their office.

- Jason Fried of the web application company 37Signals helped pioneer a "Happiness Report" that allows those on the outside to view how positive their last hundred customer service interactions were.

- Rand Fishkin of Moz, whom *Forbes* said may be "president in the world of transparency," recently posted his own performance review. All of his failures and successes from the previous year are now accessible to anyone interested.[4]

- And I even publicly share my earnings through monthly income reports posted on my website at DalePartridge.com.

As Hewlett-Packard CEO Meg Whitman says, "For any company to be successful today, it must ensure that all of the organization's stakeholders—from employees, to customers, to investors—have a clear line of sight into the company's strategy and performance, good or bad."[5]

People-over-profit leaders and organizations have opted for transparency because they know it frees. It frees them to do business unhampered. It frees them to reinvest the time they would otherwise spend trying to keep secrets. It frees them to live without the weight of trying to ensure that the right people know the right things and the wrong things stay in the shadows. And it also frees consumers to do business without having to speculate about whether they are getting the full picture.

Are you willing to find new ways to be more open with those on the inside and outside of your organization? If so, you're ready to join the companies that are breaking the system and thriving in today's marketplace.

EVERYONE CAN SEE

You may have the idea that you have a choice whether or not to be open, but in the digital age, you don't. In a world with ubiquitous access to the Internet, organizational transparency is a necessity, not an option. Why? Because today nearly everything you communicate can be fact-checked on the spot. In a globalized, interconnected era, nothing can be hidden forever.[6] And those who *aren't* open books are the ones who stick out.

Additionally, in a social-media–saturated world, transparency is assumed. The public knows everything about everyone—their current location, what they had for breakfast, photos of their new car or new baby or old dog. When businesses don't reflect the same level of transparency that the public receives from everyone else in their everyday lives, it undermines trust and cultivates consumer skepticism.

When transparency is lacking, speculation is abundant. If you're not open with others, they will naturally assume you have something to hide. And when people are uncertain, people talk. So the selective sharing of information or the refusal to allow others access is one of the fastest ways to create negative brand buzz. Building an openhanded rather than closefisted company turns out to be a great business strategy.

Sounds simple, doesn't it?

It's not, actually.

The recipe for transparency is one part vulnerability and one part accessibility. Both are costly ingredients and difficult to come by. The word *vulnerable* conjures images of a knight without his armor or a turtle lying on his back in the middle of the interstate. Companies prefer to be strong, safe, protected. But in business, vulnerability works differently than in other realms of life. When you're willing to share wins *and* losses, successes *and* failures, you'll build more trust and loyalty among your core customers. In this way, being weak will make you stronger.

Once you've added vulnerability, you need to toss in accessibility. And not just a pinch. The recipe calls for heaps of the stuff. This, too, is difficult for most companies because the more accessibility you grant to others the more control you forfeit, and companies love control. But vulnerability without accessibility is counterproductive.

For example, if you're a fast-food company that decides to release the nutrition information of your menu items, don't bury it sixteen pages deep into your website. When people attempt to find it, you'll communicate something about yourself that you might not even intend: that you're trying to hide something. The same is true for cell-phone and credit-card contracts. These organizations bury important details in a swampland of legalese. Sure, they made the information available. Technically. But they know that no one is going to read carefully enough to find it. When the hidden language is used to penalize the customer later on, trust is lost.

VULNERABILITY + ACCESSIBILITY = TRANSPARENCY

Of course, you don't have to tell everything in order to be transparent. Businesses *can't* tell everything. Some things are proprietary. Coca-Cola can't post its recipe online. A restaurant owner can't post the ingredients in their hundred-year-old secret sauce. Financial advisors can't give away the algorithm they use for successfully investing money.

Organizations must challenge the outdated thinking that creates protected silos of information. Instead, they must enter into the new normal of business that gives away as much as possible without compromising the ability to operate.

OPEN FROM THE INSIDE OUT

When Sevenly launched, I wanted transparency to be a cornerstone of the way we conducted business and interacted with the people we believed mattered so much. Openness often starts inside and works its way out, so we positioned the majority of our employees in an open workspace—nicknamed "the bullpen"—in the center of the building. A few of our employees work from offices, which we constructed from glass. Even our conference room is made of glass. Someone can still close their door and have a private conversation, but the conversation will be seen. Visibility communicates transparency.

After launching, we instituted a companywide town-hall meeting every two weeks. We huddle together in a circle—there is no platform or head of the table for those in charge—and look one another in the eyes. Any employee can ask any question of any other team member—including me—and get an answer in a public forum.

Is this always comfortable or fun? No way. I don't always like people asking me how financially stable our books are or whether they have job security. But after the meeting ends, I always feel better about having answered those difficult questions. It's freeing.

The electronic payment processing company Square holds a similar meeting each week. They call it Town Square, and they, too, allow anyone to ask anything they wish. And when they hire new staff members, they have an onboarding

A lack of transparency results in distrust and a deep sense of insecurity.

——

Dalai Lama

process called Square One, where they share what many would call sensitive information.

We also opt for openness with our customers at Sevenly. Each year, we join companies such as Ben and Jerry's, Kickstarter, and Warby Parker by releasing an exhaustive annual business report. It is a ten- to fifteen-page document that tells our consumers how many employees we have, what our age ranges are, the male-to-female ratio of our staff, how much money we gave away, how many charities we partnered with, how many people visited our website, how much growth we had on social media, what the most and least successful campaigns were, and what the most and least popular products were. We're not a public company, so we don't have to provide any of this. We do it willingly because we want to be open with our community.

This report isn't always glowing, but we don't censor or edit it to make ourselves look good. In fact, we quietly hope the report will have some glaring negatives. Why? Because negative information builds mountains of trust. Customers know that a company is being radically open when they share things that are not in the company's best interest to share.

Constructing a culture of transparency is like building a house. It happens little by little. No one expects you to have shingles hung and three coats of paint by sunrise. But the companies who will thrive in today's economy are those that are always thinking of the next step toward a more completely open company. And as they increase transparency, a new level of success is usually not far behind.

8

AUTHENTICITY ATTRACTS

Ice clinks inside your glass as you lift it toward your lips. You take a swig of the creamy, tan liquid. It's sweet and smooth. A perfect after-dinner drink.

You're drinking Baileys Original Irish Cream. You're sipping on authenticity.

Since launching in 1974, Baileys has remained authentically Irish. In fact, its Irishness is the secret ingredient in the company's recipe for success.

"It's hugely important," Baileys' external affairs director Peter O'Connor said. "We could produce Baileys more cheaply in

New Zealand or Australia, but whenever we've researched the idea consumers say 'over my dead body.'"[1]

Baileys is manufactured by Gilbeys of Ireland. Approximately 275 million liters of Irish milk from 40,000 Irish cows are used each year to produce the cream. They are top-bred Irish dairy cows that graze on 1,500 accredited Irish farms. Their marketing and labels harken back to the old country because Baileys embraces who they are. If you don't like Irish, you don't like Baileys.

Their commitment to authenticity has paid off. Baileys has become the world's top liqueur brand on sale in 180 countries, wherever alcohol is legally consumed. They account for over 50 percent of all spirits exported from Ireland, and more than 2,300 glasses of Baileys are consumed every minute of every day of every month of every year.[2]

Klipsch, an audio speaker company, is another organization that has found success from just being who they are. Founded by Paul Klipsch in 1946, the company first operated out of a tin shed in Hope, Arkansas. Paul's goal was to "produce the excitement of a live orchestra performance in his living room" through horn-loaded technology.[3]

But that was nearly seventy years ago. Today, many audio companies cater to tweens looking for colorful (probably plastic) gadgets. Klipsch resisted the temptation to get sidetracked by these fleeting trends. "We feel that the whole market is so crowded," says Paul Jacobs, Klipsch's CEO. "This is authentic to who we really are when we quit being someone else."[4]

Authenticity is a collection of choices that we have to make every day. It's about the choice to show up and be real. The choice to be honest. The choice to let our true selves be seen.

Brené
Brown

The company continues to focus on producing high-fidelity audio products, holding fast to their founder's nonnegotiables. Their "no-bull—just-great-products" marketing approach has generated sassy taglines such as "Pissing off the neighbors since 1946" and "Stop buying crap audio. It's embarrassing."[5]

Though Klipsch has continued to innovate throughout the years, they've refused to change their tune and have been even more successful as a result. As the Klipsch website promises, "Klipsch still looks to the future with an eye to the past. Everything Klipsch does today and 100 years from now will reflect Paul's no-compromise spirit and the brand's commitment to delivering the world's most powerful, detailed and emotional sound reproduction."[6]

From sips to sounds, the companies that are most true to themselves are the ones that succeed in today's marketplace.

ACCEPT WHO YOU ARE

Authenticity is a simple concept, really. It's just living your message. Practicing what you preach. Being who you are. But developing this trait takes time and requires discipline. Here are four waypoints in the path to authenticity that attracts.

Discover your organizational personality.

You can't be what you are if you don't know who you are. What are the unique talents and passions of your team members? What does your organization value above all else? If you were forced to eliminate programs and line items, which ones would be the last to go? What wakes your team up in the morning and keeps them up at night? What do you do well, and how do you like to do it, and why?

WHAT ARE YOU DOING CURRENTLY THAT IS NOT YOU? MURDER IT. WRESTLE IT TO THE GROUND, STRANGLE THE LIFE OUT OF IT, AND BURY IT IN YOUR BACKYARD.

These questions will help you begin to understand the personality of your company. If you aren't sure, interview your staff to see how they describe the organization. If your team gives roughly the same answers, you may be further along than you suspected. If there are as many variations as there are job titles, you probably have your work cut out for you.

Once you discover your organizational personality, invest more time and resources in projects that align with who you are and less in those tasks that run counter to your identity. Eventually, you should get to a point where you have complete company alignment with your organizational personality. What are you doing currently that is not you? Murder it. Wrestle it to the ground, strangle the life out of it, and bury it in your backyard. Stop investing in things that are not you.

Resist the urge to be something else.

Where many companies get into trouble is that they attempt to manufacture authenticity rather than *be* authentic. They hire market research companies to help determine which language to use when they speak and which images to utilize in their advertising. They attempt to create a corporate personality that they believe will appeal to consumers—to be all things to all people. But a brand doesn't feel real when it tries too hard to be real.

Brands tend to be too programmed, too perfect, too plastic. But you're not going to fool anyone. Human beings have an uncanny ability to sniff out deception. People-over-profit companies know this, which is why they resist the urge to become something else just because it seems more marketable.

When we allow people to know us—personally, professionally, organizationally—we attract new followers and instill loyalty in those we already have. But when we try to fake it, we create distrust.

"If we sense that a person or a company is acting primarily out of self-interest—if they tell us something because they want something from us like a vote or a purchase, for example—then we raise an eyebrow, grow suspicious and keep our distance," says leadership guru Simon Sinek. "If they tell us something because they genuinely believe it and want to help us . . . then we actually respect and trust them more."[7]

Authenticity is the act of telling people what you believe and care about, not telling them what you think they want you to believe or care about.

Help others become who they are.

Business is really just the act of stewarding a series of

relationships. So if you want to create a culture of authenticity, your work should help those you serve become who they are too.

One organization that does this well is the clothing retailer Anthropologie. Rather than create a rigid sketch of a demographic and implement a one-size-fits-all marketing plan, they've encouraged associates at all levels to dig deep into understanding the thirtysomething married woman in the communities where their stores operate and then create environments where those customers can get in touch with who they are.

There is no corporate standard for an Anthropologie retail store. The decor in each location is curated by local designers who fill the space with found objects and antiques. Is this more expensive than shipping mass-produced displays approved by a higher-up in a faraway corporate office? You bet. But "it creates a sense of authenticity that resonates with the brand's local devotees."[8]

The goal is to create a space where their customers, who may be juggling a career, kids, and other responsibilities, can get in touch with the adventurous, bohemian woman who lives inside but rarely gets to come out and stretch her legs. No wonder customers often spend over an hour and close to eighty dollars per visit in Anthropologie retail stores. Not too shabby for a company that doesn't advertise.[9]

You will be a successful organization if you can learn to be true to yourself while empowering customers to be who they are. Help your customers love and embrace themselves, and you'll offer them a beautiful gift they'll not soon forget.

Continue to innovate, even as you remain true to yourself.

Embracing authenticity can sometimes be a bit like walking a tightrope. To remain true to itself, a brand must remain committed to its values. And yet, if the company wants to stay relevant, it must become as dynamic as change itself. A people-over-profit brand must balance these conflicting impulses, finding ways to be original without becoming a sellout.

Companies evolve just like humans age. But even though time will bring wrinkles and age spots, it won't change your skeletal shape. You'll never wake up to discover that a leg has been replaced by a flipper. (If this happens, consult a doctor or veterinarian immediately.) Some things don't change with age because they are part of what makes you who you are as a human being.

The same is true for organizations. You must identify which parts of you make you who you are and which parts should remain flexible. Name your nonnegotiables. These are the timeless components of your company that should never change. What are those elements of your organizational personality that aren't for sale? Once you know what is not negotiable, you'll be able to evolve without selling out. There is a difference between innovating and compromising. Learn to do the former while avoiding the latter.

It starts with you.

You can't have an authentic company if you don't have authentic people working for and leading that company. This is one of the beliefs I struggle most to live out. I started multiple companies in my early twenties, but Sevenly was my first chance to live out what I really believed I was good at: raising funding and awareness for the world's greatest causes. I'm philanthropic, but I'm also an entrepreneur. I wanted to believe that I was the guy in Africa walking through a crowd of laughing children. But that wasn't me. It wasn't true to who I was.

So authenticity is a struggle for me every day. I change the way I dress and adjust the subjects I speak about to impress others. As a boss, I have deep flaws even though I try to mask them to project the spitting image of a young, successful entrepreneur. I'm tempted daily—no, hourly—to make my social media feed the highlight reel of my life.

But you know what? I'm a workaholic. I'm often a mediocre husband. I'm not a perfect boss or even always a good one. Some of my flaws are so defective that I've had to seek professional counseling. I'm not as cool as my pictures online make me out to be, not as wise as my Twitter feed makes me sound, and not as important as writing this book makes me appear.

But in order to grow an authentic company, I need to learn to be an authentic leader. And you must do the same.

Become who you are.

People Over Profit

FIGHT THE LIE

The temptation to be inauthentic is especially strong when it comes to social causes. Many companies are profit-focused with a charitable cause tacked on. When Sevenly launched, we decided to conduct business differently. We didn't want to market a fabricated reality—to pretend that we were the most altruistic group of people who ever walked the globe—but rather show others that we were a bunch of passionate folks who hoped to accomplish a little good in the world. Sevenly is a community of people like you who have gathered around a common cause.

That's why "People matter" is integrated into everything we do. When you enter our office, the phrase "People matter" is plastered on a five-foot-by-five-foot chalkboard. It's been on many of our products. It is on our website, business cards, and e-mail signatures. We don't want anyone to forget who we are. We're like a transponder sending out a constant signal with the "People matter" message. As ships pick up our message, the ones that agree with it sail toward us.

But we don't want just to spread our mission; we want to share our personality. That's why the pictures on the team page of our web site are fun. We share interesting facts about ourselves and make goofy faces. We embrace the nuances of our staff's personalities. We want people to know who we are. The pet clothes on our website even feature our own dogs as models. Whenever we have an opportunity to add a personal element, we do.

Another place we work to promote authenticity is in our videos. We rotate team members in our videos, making sure there is always a real Sevenly employee in almost every one. If an employee is passionate about a particular charity we're working with, we'll let them take the lead in that production.

We even showcase the inner workings of our company and the good humor of our team on social media. If you follow Sevenly on Facebook or Twitter or Instagram, you'll see pictures of our team members doing what they love. We highlight the funny, hand-drawn unicorn on the office refrigerator to show people that we know how to laugh. We celebrate and grieve publicly.

As easy as all this sounds, it requires bravery to accept who you are and stop trying to be what you think people want. But in a world overloaded with sales pitches and hollow slogans, it is worth it. Being authentic will save you money and build a stronger, more loyal community of stakeholders.

So go ahead. Be yourself.

9

QUALITY SPEAKS

Some say the air in Austin, Texas, is a mix of dust and magic. Todd Sanders would probably agree.

During his sophomore year in college in 1992, Sanders ended up there after taking a wrong turn on the highway. A graphic design major who was enamored by custom signage, Sanders fell in love with what he saw in the city that's famous for being weird.

"We were driving around town, and within 15 minutes—20 tops—I said, 'I'm going to move here, and I am going to build neon signs,'" Sanders recalls.[1]

Months later, he packed up and moved to the quirky Texas

town to become an artist and entrepreneur. Though he was eager to get started, he had a vision to produce the highest quality signs around. This meant spending a decade perfecting his craft, including a three-year apprenticeship in a local neon shop.

Sanders sacrificed much for his vision. He was forced to live in a trailer with no electricity on a ranch outside of town and made $300 a week for years.

"My dad would come and see me, and later he told me that one time he saw me sitting in a chair in the yard with the cows walking all around, and he just started crying," Sanders says. "He couldn't believe I was doing all of that for my art."[2]

Sanders continued to hone his craft and improve his designs, shifting his focus away from commercial signage to producing custom art pieces inspired by vintage signs from the 1930s and '40s. He draws inspiration from a stack of more than four hundred trade journals, graphic posters, and books. Every piece begins with a hand-drawn rendering and then is battered and built in his backyard.

"Sometimes, at night, I sit in the backyard and when it's all lit up, and I'm experiencing the glow of the neon and the line art and even the flashing bulbs, it's almost a spiritual experience," he says.[3]

But Sanders isn't the only one who's been deeply moved by the handcrafted signs. His company, Roadhouse Relics, has a four-month waiting list, and his art pieces have been featured in national publications, such as *Fortune* and *Esquire*, and in the films of Terrence Malick and Robert Rodriguez. Committing to craftsmanship turned out to be the most lucrative choice of his life.

But quality isn't just a virtue that works for artists with small boutique businesses. Consider Umpqua, a regional bank based in Oregon with fewer than a hundred locations. In 2001, Umpqua set out to reimagine their banking experience. They built a list of what was important to their customers, and what mattered most to them as an organization.

Umpqua discovered that their customers craved a quality, intimate banking experience. They'd grown weary of national bank brands' impersonal, unsympathetic, and efficiency-obsessed customer service. That's why they chose this smaller bank in the first place.

So Umpqua executives decided to make a radical shift. They implemented a "slow banking" experience, promising a level of comfort and personal service that bigger banks had long since abandoned. Their flagship store opened in Portland's Pearl District and received $1 million in deposits in its first month, and a record $50 million in deposits after nine months.[4] Umpqua's website declares they are the "world's greatest bank," and people in the communities they serve increasingly agree.

Todd Sanders' Roadhouse Relics and Umpqua Bank teach two lessons. First, committing to fanatical quality gives an organization a competitive edge because it speaks about how much you value customers. It speaks about who you are and what sets you apart, and the level of excellence they can expect. People will drive farther, make sacrifices, and often pay top dollar for superior service and craftsmanship.

Second, Sanders and Umpqua teach us that quality builds credibility. The aesthetic of your website design or the way your products are packaged or even the stock of paper used in your business cards will shape whether or not customers think you are a credible company. If these elements are excellent, people think, *If they care* this *much about the smallest details, then they care about me.* When you commit to quality, customers will recognize that you care more about them than more callous competitors, and offer you their business instead.

A PAINFUL PROFIT

Quality is a value that most business leaders will say is important, but they are frightened to death about actually committing to it. Why? Because increasing quality may mean increasing prices or decreasing profit margins. I can empathize because I fight this fear too. Sevenly products aren't the most expensive goods on the market. But they aren't the cheapest either. You can find a lower priced T-shirt or backpack or water bottle or poster at any big-box store on Main Street.

I worry from time to time that we won't be able to capture the tens of millions of price-conscious consumers saturating the American marketplace. But I'm more afraid of making subtle compromises in quality, or that we'll end up selling our soul for thirty pieces of silver.

To protect ourselves, Sevenly takes stock of our standards often. We want to fight for quality, and we always ask, "How can we make our products better?" I have a running document—the Sevenly Quality Inventory—where I keep tabs on everything our company possesses and puts out. This list is a record of what is achieving the highest quality and what needs to be improved. By evaluating our business in this way, I've identified four aspects of quality that every leader must focus on and every consumer will notice.

1. Physical Quality

Anything a customer or team member can touch should be excellent. At Sevenly, we consider the quality of paper we print on, the inks we use on garments, and the level of recyclable content in the packages we ship. Before we'll print on a T-shirt, tank top, or hoodie, we survey the cotton blends and order samples so we can see how the fabric hangs and feel it against our skin.

We've sold half a million products through Sevenly. If I poured money into marketing and advertising and slick design, but the products we sell fell apart shortly after arrival, then all that money would be wasted. If the shirt falls apart or the bag unravels or the flask rusts, customers will not only never buy from us again but also will tell their friends not to buy from us. Quality is the best marketing. As of the writing of this sentence, the average Sevenly customer will buy 2.8 times a year with an annual customer value of $112.

We even hand draw our printables. This is more expensive, but originality is important to us. We feel computers have eliminated the beauty of craftsmanship, so we make the investment. Our desire is for Sevenly to be a place where you can buy products you like that support causes you love. Sometimes a people-over-profit mindset begins as product-over-profit thinking.

Since our team members are as valuable as our customers, we also make sure they are equipped with top-shelf supplies. We issue quality pens, desks, and computers. We even consider the comfortability of our office chairs. At Sevenly, everyone gets the same business cards I have. They're printed on thick chipboard with two-toned edges and a beautifully embossed "People matter."

Take inventory of the physical objects throughout your office. What do these items communicate to your employees about the value you place on them? Now survey the quality and durability of the products you provide to customers. Do these items indicate that you care more about customers or profit margins?

2. Experiential Quality

Craftsmanship is not just tangible but also emotional. Customers don't only purchase products; they also buy an experience. (If you don't believe me, ask Apple.) Many companies, however, never consider the experiences they are creating.

A good example of an organization that has made strides in this type of quality is Virgin America, who has improved the flying experience with Red, an in-flight customer interface. Red enables passengers to do more than watch movies and TV shows. They can also order food and drinks "at straight-forward prices, with a 'real-time' understanding of what is available, the ability to customize, and therefore the bonus of receiving your order more quickly and with less effort."[5] No more waiting for the lumbering drink cart to make its way to you only to find out they've run out of club soda.

At Sevenly, when we decide to develop a new product, we pick a cause and then search for the charity that does the very best work in that space. Once we agree on a partner charity, we brainstorm the phrase that would best communicate this cause. We've used, "Autism: different not less" and "Someone's praying for the things you take for granted" and "Be someone who makes someone else look forward to tomorrow." We test these phrases on social media and let our community respond.

When we've settled on a phrase, it is handed to our art department. They make five to ten iterations of concepts. Once a direction is selected, they sketch every letter and image on paper, often with an ink-dipped pen. We then vectorize the art, create color variations, and hand it off to the production team, who tests it on various sample garments. The product is given to our photography team, who creates optimal lighting and takes stunning pictures with top-of-the-line cameras.

After customers purchase our products, we ship them in quality packaging and include information about the cause they are supporting in the shipment. When our customers view the product picture online or receive a Sevenly package in the mail, we hope the experience—not just the final product—communicates a commitment to craftsmanship.

If you work in a store that customers visit, what kind of experience are you creating in this space? If you're selling goods, what does the packaging communicate? Is the atmosphere in your office one that encourages creativity and builds loyalty among your team?

3. Visual Quality

The twenty-first century is an aesthetic era. The way you look in an interview can determine whether or not you get the

Don't compromise.

People Over Profit

#PeopleOverProfit

job. You may not let your child play with a neighbor because the other kid's appearance unsettles you. The visual presentation of a billboard or commercial can influence whether you patronize a business or visit a website. Colors and fonts and layouts have never meant more than they do now.

In our current age, visual elements are no longer representations of the brand but an expression of the brand's heart. So design must be a core value of any organization. Whenever something has your name or fingerprints attached, it can't be less than great. Visual design is the first touch point most people will have with your company. It can dictate the rest of your relationship. So make sure you stack your creative team with all-stars.

At Sevenly, we have a forty-page brand guide that has a glossary of terms we commonly use, terms we don't use, ways our logo can and cannot be used, and our creative values. It is a Bible and backbone to us.

Ask a few creative friends who will speak honestly with you to evaluate your website, printed materials, and logos. Then ask them what these visual components communicate about your organization. You may be surprised by what you find out.

4. Personal Quality

As the world has become more automated, few things communicate excellence like a personal touch. Your organization should be dreaming up new ways to personally interact with your community. Call or even visit one of your customers without an agenda and see if it doesn't make an impression.

Recently, Sevenly integrated a new shipping system. A bug forced us to delay distribution, and several thousand orders were late as a result. We could have ignored it or sent a mass e-mail, but instead we divvied up the names and addresses of those who were affected. Our team took the time to hand-write apologies to each one. Some raving fans were created as a result of a potentially disastrous calamity.

We also host events at our office a few times per year where we invite the community to come and feel us out. We let them wander through our office, surveying our artwork and products. We bring in the best food trucks and offer cold beer. (Not cheapo American light beer, either. The tasty, craft kind from a local brewery.) We'll often have a well-known speaker or live music. At these events, people can see and touch and taste and hear what we believe in. It becomes an echo chamber of physical, experiential, and visual quality with a personal touch. Oh, and one more thing: we don't charge a dime for any of it.

Are you content to engage your customers from a distance? What about your team members? How can you become more personal as an organization?

EARS TO HEAR

One way to ensure that you are pursuing a high level of

excellence is by creating a culture of evaluation and feed-back. Quality isn't what *you* say it is; it's what *they* say it is. You're biased because it is your idea, and cutting quality may put more money in your pocket. Human minds have an uncanny ability to rationalize poor decisions.

We've built a survey culture at Sevenly. We send out surveys regularly to customers via our social media platforms. We also e-mail a large general survey to our customers and our partner charities quarterly, making sure they are pleased. We even send out anonymous surveys to our staff. Collecting this feedback has made an immeasurable difference in quality.

We once ordered a thousand tri-blend cotton shirts, which are some of the most comfortable shirts on the market. Thanks to survey responses, we learned that one of our garments was shrinking when we were heating it up to dry the ink because of the blend. So when the customers received these shirts, they were not fitting optimally. Actually, that is an under-statement. It turned a grown man's shirt into a midriff.

When the survey responses were brought to my attention, I walked over to our printer to observe the drying process. I measured the garments by hand before and after to determine which temperatures were causing the vertical shrinkage. In the end, we had to select a different shirt. Thanks to the sur-veys, we recognized the problem early and avoided placing an order for another three thousand units the following week.

But conducting surveys will be a meaningless waste of time if you don't respond to feedback. Cell-phone companies, for example, often ask customers who call for support to respond to a "short survey." But these companies aren't responding to the feedback. They aren't listening. They aren't improving. So callers have learned to decline the survey when offered. Quality means listening, responding, and making changes *quickly*.

We found out once that an ink we were using had formaldehyde in it. It was fine when you set it out for retail, but after it was shipped in a sealed bag and then opened up, it smelled horrible. When multiple surveys indicated our clothes smelled like dead fish, we knew we had a quality problem. We would never have had any idea otherwise because we don't ship stuff to ourselves. Within hours of noticing the problem, our team was in an emergency meeting. Within days, we were scouring for solutions. Within a week, we had implemented a change.

Take time to develop a system for collecting feedback from everyone your company touches. When you receive feedback, take it seriously and respond quickly. Few other changes have the potential to increase your organization's excellence as quickly as this can.

DON'T GIVE UP THE FIGHT

What do you do if you work for an established company that you feel no longer values quality like they used to or should? Large and mature companies are big ships that are tedious to turn. Is it too late? Should you jump ship before you lose your sanity in pursuit of a lost cause?

No. It is never too late to course correct.

Consider the motorcycle company Harley-Davidson. Today, they are the most reliable motorcycle manufacturer and one of the most recognizable brands in America. But in the 1980s, Harley-Davidson was teetering on bankruptcy because of the slipping quality of their products. That's when higher-ups started to get serious about returning to their roots by improving standards. They decided to create a better product.

"In 1982, Harley-Davidson had no money of its own," chairman Richard Teerlink told Harvard MBA students in 2003. "We were $90 million in debt, and bankers weren't willing to loan us a penny. We had a good brand and loyal customers, but we weren't generating a profit because we didn't have a quality product at that point. We had to improve the quality of our product to be fair to the customer. If we hadn't improved the reliability of Harley-Davidson products, the company wouldn't be here today."[6]

People-over-profit companies know that few things create trust and loyalty and communicate corporate values to customers more than excellence. Whether you're a household name that's been in existence for a century or a fresh-faced community bank or some guy banging on metal in his backyard, it's not too late to commit to quality.

Never settle for satisfactory.

10

GENEROSITY RETURNS

Did your mom ever tell you that if you didn't study hard in school and eat your vegetables you'd wind up flipping burgers? Patrick Terry prayed for that outcome.

In 2005, Terry decided to open a different kind of burger joint that would reimagine the way the American staple is sold. P. Terry's Burger Stand was founded in Austin, Texas, and quickly became known as an "anti-fast food chain." Sure, they sold hamburgers, french fries, milkshakes, and everything else you might expect. But glance under the hood of this organization and you'll find they aren't like other quick-service restaurants.

P. Terry's uses only quality ingredients—including all-natural beef—and is committed to customer service. Their operations are eco-friendly, which includes recycling paper and cardboard behind each store. And yet, they still manage to keep prices low. Their hamburger sells for about two bucks.

These distinctives alone are enough to set the chain apart from the local Burger King, but what really makes P. Terry's special is their commitment to generosity. Their team members are paid well above minimum wage, they offer English classes to Spanish-speaking employees, they give interest-free emergency loans to people needing an apartment or automobile, and they always promote from within.[1] P. Terry's offers their employees a bonus at the end of each year—$65,000 was paid out in December 2013. And if that weren't enough, the burger chain has donated more than $330,000 to local causes.

Has Patrick's generous strategy worked out? They have nine locations and counting and more than three hundred employees, so I'd say so.

P. Terry's isn't the only company trying to give more away. There's always TOMS Shoes, the footwear company that pioneered a one-for-one model where every pair of shoes purchased provides a pair for a child in need. Warby Parker, an eyeglass company, does the same with spectacles, and Australia-based Baby Teresa employs a one-for-one model with infant clothes. Nordstrom recently opened a test store where all profits go to charity, and Starbucks has a handful of coffee shops where a big chunk of the profits is donated to the needy.[2]

Every organization today seems to be wracking their brains for ways to give more. But some companies donate to *appear* generous rather than build it into their DNA. This temptation makes generosity a tricky virtue; but if done well and honestly, creating a culture of generosity can propel your organization to even greater success.

GENEROSITY IS NOT SOMETHING AN ORGANIZATION DOES; IT'S SOMETHING AN ORGANIZATION IS. MANY COMPANIES GET INTO TROUBLE BECAUSE THEY DON'T UNDERSTAND THE DIFFERENCE.

_____

AN OPENHANDED SYSTEM

Generosity is not something an organization does; it's something an organization is. Many companies get into trouble because they don't understand the difference.

Generosity should be selfless, not conditional.

The primary impulse of business is the opposite of generosity. Business is all about receiving; it's about profit; it's about reciprocity. By contrast, generosity is selfless. It is giving without expecting anything in return. It's built on love and care and compassion.

Wharton professor Adam Grant, in his book *Give and Take*, says most people fall into one of three categories:

> **Givers:** Seek to give away with no expectation of receiving in return

Takers: Don't give; are only in business for themselves

Matchers: Give to receive something in return[3]

Grant found that givers tend to be the most successful because they are able to cultivate a network of raving fans who want to support their way of doing business. Who would've guessed?

Many organizations don't recognize this. They play the short game and make the grave mistake of trying to use "generosity" as a marketing tool. They give so that they'll look charitable or honorable or to make consumers feel good about doing business with them. But they do not realize this behavior can come across as disingenuous, inauthentic, and even manipulative. By trying to appear philanthropic, the company ends up looking like a snake-oil salesman. Oh, the irony.

Our goal at Sevenly is to lead a generation toward generosity. This begins with the way we treat our team. On a new hire's first day, he or she is handed a gift box, which includes a welcome letter from the CEO, a set of "People matter" notebooks, three gift cards to take fellow staff members out for lunch, a *StrengthsFinder* book, a shirt in their size, and a gift certificate to Sevenly for a friend that they can give away. They get an office tour, have lunch with our culture and community development director, and are issued a brand-new Apple computer. Then they sit down to begin work, knowing that they're being paid more than the industry standard for their job and have a considerable benefits package.

We learned from a survey that the thing people wanted

most was free drinks, so we provide our team with unlimited coffee, tea, and Vitamin Water and bake fresh cookies almost every day. We even give our employees a stipend for Mother's Day and Father's Day to invest in their most important relationships.

Our hope is to model generosity for our team so they will be more charitable in their personal lives. That's why we offer free financial planning and tax consulting to employees. We understand that finances often limit generosity and can cause stress in our lives. We want to help them live the best quality of life possible and never feel restricted from giving.

Because we give seven dollars of every item purchased, generosity is embedded into our business transactions. We give away 22 percent of our gross revenue, and in 2012 alone, we gave away five times our net profit. It makes no sense, but it works.

I realize that the Sevenly business model makes generosity sound easy. Some organizations have thousands of employees, hundred-year histories, and a complex web of procedures that won't allow for the full implementation of our philosophy. But every company (and individual, for that matter) can afford to give something. If you're waiting for the perfect time to give, it will never happen—because the "perfect time" is a myth, a fairy tale, a legend. There will always be constraints, barriers, and a good excuse not to pursue generosity. You'll always have salaries and bills and vendors to pay. So if you're waiting for the perfect time, your wallet will win again and again.

No one has ever become poor by giving.

—

Anne
Frank

Instead, start small. Look for ways to build the incredible into the ordinary. Give your employees permission to perform the extraordinary and be selfless. Offer them the freedom to do for one what they wish they could do for all.

I think of a story told about Morton's Steakhouse. Peter Shankman was boarding the last leg of a multi-city flight. It was approaching dinnertime and he knew his stomach would be rumbling on the drive home from the airport. So he decided to interject some humor into this situation by sending the following tweet:

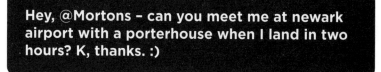

> Hey, @Mortons – can you meet me at newark airport with a porterhouse when I land in two hours? K, thanks. :)

I wish I could have seen his face when he deplaned and saw a tuxedoed gentleman with a twenty-four-ounce Morton's porterhouse steak, shrimp, potatoes, bread, napkins, and silverware. This story is even more incredible when you consider that in less than two and a half hours, a Morton's employee had to notice the Tweet, hatch the plan, get approval for the idea, have a chef cook the food, and then have someone drive more than twenty-three miles from the nearest Morton's to meet him at the right location and locate his gate.[4]

If Morton's prepared a free custom-made dinner for every hungry traveler, they'd go bankrupt. But they gave at least one employee permission to do the incredible and offer one person what they wish they could give to everyone. There's no telling how the tales of this selfless act of generosity have impacted the organization as a whole. It has been told on blogs, news sites, business journals, and now in this book. As it turns out, unconditional generosity has a way of returning to us.

Generosity should be built in, not tacked on.

This virtue works only when it is sewn into the fabric of your organizational personality. Rather than an afterthought or a reaction, generosity should be implanted in your DNA. Whenever someone from our team goes out for lunch, they fight for the check. And whenever we're meeting with a potential vendor, we often bring them a gift bag with Sevenly products inside. We're not acting this way because we want something in return. We simply hope to express a generous experience in these relationships.

When generosity is who you are rather than something you do, it will seep out of your organization's pores naturally.

Few companies have a more generous culture than the online retailer Zappos. They offer employees on-site Weight Watchers training with reimbursements, access to prepaid legal assistance, and a nap room available in case someone needs to rest and recharge. In their cafeteria, team members can choose from free sandwiches, salads, soup, cereal, and ice cream.

Zappos is also known to take exceptional care of their customers. They offer free shipping and free returns. In fact, they encourage customers to order multiple sizes and then send back the ones that don't fit. If there's a problem with an order, a team of customer service representatives in Las Vegas are available to field the calls. These employees don't read from a script, so as to provide responses tailored to actual needs. Instead, Zappos offers everyone in their call center seven weeks of training on how to make (and keep) customers happy.

A few years ago, an elderly woman had recently had some "harsh medical treatments" that left her feet numb yet sensitive to pressure. Her old shoes were now useless, so the woman's daughter logged onto Zappos and ordered her six pairs in hopes that at least one of them would be suitable. Upon arrival, the elderly lady phoned Zappos to process a return for the pairs that didn't work.

In the course of the call, the woman explained why she was returning so many items. Two days later, she received a bouquet of "get well" flowers from Zappos, and she and her daughter were upgraded to "Zappos VIP Member" status.[5] The online retailer doesn't have a written policy instructing employees to send flowers in cases like these. Generosity is just who they are.

Generosity is holistic, not just financial.

One of the biggest misconceptions about generosity is that it is primarily, if not exclusively, financial. If you believe this then your organization will only be as generous as you are prosperous. But generosity is a holistic virtue. It's rarely about money.

You can be generous with your talents. If you're a graphic designer, for example, donate your skills to help a nonprofit design a fundraising brochure. You can be generous with your time. Tutor in a local school or care for the elderly. Find community service projects where your team can volunteer together for a good cause. If a team member needs help moving or a listening ear, be there for them. You can also extend generosity through collaboration. Join forces with coworkers or, yes, even competitors to pursue a greater good. If you're generous with nonfinancial gifts, you'll become more generous in other ways too.

Molding Box is an order fulfillment, shipping, and distribution company. They've decided to be generous through their hiring practices, openly staffing their team with ex-convicts. Founder and CEO Jordan Guernsey says everyone deserves a second chance. This includes, for example, people like a Molding Box employee who is a former bank robber. This policy has helped integrate valuable workers back into society, but it also expresses an undeniable culture of generosity.

THE BELIEF THAT KEEPS ON GIVING

An ironic thing about selfless giving is that it often comes back to you anyway. When you are generous with your employees, they will be generous to you. You'll never have to worry whether they'll stay late and finish the job or speak well of you. And when you're generous with your customers, they'll return.

WHEN WE GIVE FREELY, WE'LL OFTEN FIND THAT GENEROSITY IS LESS LIKE AN ARROW AND MORE LIKE A BOOMERANG.

Gillette gives away free razors to teenagers for their first shave and captures many of them in the process. Chick-fil-A gives away astounding amounts of free sandwiches. A recent sampling study from Knowledge Networks PDI noted that sampling programs (the kind used at Costco or Sam's Club) drove a 475 percent sales lift on the day of the event.[6] Letting people taste quality products and services for free will encourage them to come back at full price.

Netflix offers consumers a one-month free trial of its service, but Wall Street was concerned about this offer when the first season of *House of Cards* was released. The series was a Netflix exclusive, expected to be wildly popular, and all thirteen episodes were released at once. Forecasters feared that consumers would sign up for the free trial, binge watch the series, and then cancel. But out of the 1.3 million people who signed up for the free trial that month, only 8,000 (0.6 percent) did this. By giving away their services for free, they generated goodwill among first-time customers.[7]

Or consider Panera Bread Company, who recently opened donations-only cafes where customers pay only what they can afford—a serious draw for the down-and-out. You might expect this would break the bank, but it hasn't. The sandwich company estimates that 60 percent of customers pay the suggested donation, 20 percent pay less, and 20 percent pay more.[8] Generosity returns.

But beware. The idea that generosity returns is a description of how the world works, not the motivation for giving. We should give because we love others, because we want to meet their needs, and because we believe that people matter. When we give freely, we'll often find that generosity is less like an arrow and more like a boomerang.

11

COURAGE SUSTAINS

Ray C. Anderson may be the most courageous business leader you've never heard of.

After recognizing a need for flexible floor coverings in the modern office environment, Anderson founded Interface in 1973. Helped by a modest investment, the organization launched with an ambitious vision and fifteen committed employees. The company reached $11 million in sales within five years and went public in 1983. Interface continued to expand, gaining entry into the European and Middle Eastern markets. After undergoing more than fifty acquisitions, they became the world's largest producer of modular carpet with manufacturing on four continents and sales in more than 110 countries.[1]

At this point in a company's history, most founding CEOs would flip the cruise control switch and enjoy the fruits of their labor. But Anderson had an epiphany in the mid-1990s that the company should be committed to not just profit but also people, process, product, and place. He cast a radical vision for redirecting the company toward a new set of goals, challenging them to embrace fresh thinking and a revamped business model.

Implementing such sweeping changes was not easy for a CEO of a company that dealt in synthetic materials, such as nylon, and was heavily dependent on petrochemicals. Anderson faced intense backlash even as he assembled a task force to help implement his plan.

"His words sparked tears, anger, defensiveness and fierce intellectual challenge," recalled Jim Hartzfeld, who led the task force.[2] Some of the members even suggested that the Interface chairman had lost his grip on reality.

But Anderson held his ground and persuaded the staff to his position with passionate pleas and compelling vision casting. "We are all part of the continuum of humanity and life," he said after his epiphany. "We will have lived our brief span and either helped or hurt that continuum and the earth that sustains all life. It's that simple. Which will it be?"[3]

To their credit, Interface investors and stakeholders eventually followed the iconoclastic industrialist's lead, and his bold plan was set in motion.

Interface integrated the belief that people matter.

As their mission statement now says, "We will strive to create an organization wherein all people are accorded unconditional respect and dignity; one that allows each person to continuously learn and develop."[4] They began focusing more on the happiness of the Interface staff—including flattening much of their organizational structure—which led to *Fortune* naming the organization one of the "100 Best Companies to Work For."

Interface integrated the belief that truth wins.

They began speaking honestly about how the carpet industry had become environmentally irresponsible, including its overuse of petrochemicals and excessive waste. The company admitted being a part of the problem—Interface factories produced hundreds of gallons of waste water and almost a thousand pollutants—and they vowed to do better.

Interface integrated the belief that transparency frees.

They committed to what they called "Mission Zero," which was a goal of eliminating any negative impact their company had on the environment by 2020. To remain accountable, they selected transparency as one of their company values and released web pages where customers could track their progress. From 1996 to 2012, Interface went from 1 percent recycled and bio-based material use to 49 percent, nearly cut their greenhouse gas emissions in half, increased renewable energy to 36 percent, and slashed their landfill waste and water use.[5]

Interface integrated the belief that authenticity attracts.

The company embraces the personality of its founder and has become innovative, risky, and bold. No other floor covering company is quite like Interface, and they like it that way.

Interface integrated the belief that quality speaks.

They added the following to their new mission statement: "We will focus on product (which includes service) through constant emphasis on process quality and engineering, which we will combine with careful attention to our customers' needs so as always to deliver superior value to our customers, thereby maximizing all stakeholders' satisfaction."[6] Interface continues to be an industry leader in developing and integrating new technologies. Their product quality exceeds industry standards, which has earned Interface dozens of national awards.[7]

Interface integrated the belief that generosity returns.

Conducting business as usual may have been more profitable in the short term, but Interface was playing the long game. They made generous investments into better processes and products with a lower environmental impact. In addition, they have grown more generous with employees, expanding

Be always sure you're right— then go ahead.

— Davy Crockett

benefits packages and offering tuition reimbursement so team members can pursue educational goals.

Ray C. Anderson died at the age of 77 in 2011 after battling cancer for nearly two years. The avowed "recovering plunderer" left behind a $1.1 billion carpet company that is still revolutionizing its industry and has launched an accompanying foundation in his name that continues to make large donations to worthy causes. But more than anything, Anderson left behind a legacy of courage—a testament to what can happen if one will only dare to dream of a better world.

FEAR SUCKS

Whenever you are on the cusp of making a decision that requires courage—whether it is launching a company or asking a girl out—a devilish creature is usually hiding around the corner, waiting for the perfect opportunity to lean over your shoulder and whisper in your ear. His name is Fear, and he will remind you that the decision is not practical, convenient, economical, or sensible. You knew these things going into it, of course, but somehow it sounds more ominous when Fear says it. (Perhaps a bold idea popped into your head while reading this chapter, but Fear is already talking you out of it.)

I've had several rendezvous with this crippling naysayer as a business leader. Fear was an easy emotion to play with when I was a single entrepreneur living in a tiny apartment. But today, I have a wife and a child and a mortgage and an office and employees who count on me. I now battle fright daily.

Fear comes in various forms, depending on what we're facing and what stage of life we're in. Here are some of its most common shapes.

Fear of Change

The reason we consistently operate a particular way is because we've convinced ourselves that our procedures, policies, and personnel have made us successful. If you're a liar, you lie because you think it makes you successful. If you're deceptive but profitable, you've probably attributed your success to your business practices. Every dollar you make becomes a reason *not* to change. But even if poor habits have earned you a few extra bucks, they are still unsustainable.

Tradition is powerful. Pattern is powerful. Consistency is powerful. But when they are deceptive or destructive, they become prisons and ultimately executioners. You'll eventually either have to change or become obsolete.

Fear of Failure

You may be saying, "Okay, Dale. This works for you and for Sevenly. But I don't know that it will work for me and my business." First, I think good morals make for great business no matter who you are, where you live, when you were born, or what line of work you are in. But beyond that, we must be honest with each other:

You.

May.

Fail.

But you should never be ashamed for fighting for better business practices, for a better system, for a better world. Becoming a people-over-profit organization is not just about success. It is about the world we live in and the people who live in it with us. We are influencers, stewards, and change makers. These types of people fail and fail often. But they learn from their mistakes and press on.

Fear of Admitting Fault

Few acts are as painful as apologies. But admitting where and when we've been wrong is critical to moving forward. I recently admitted to investors that I've made a mistake by failing to diversify. The words were difficult to speak because I wanted them to see me as competent. But it was the right thing to do.

When Apple released its program Maps, users found the product to be inferior to the previous Google Maps integration. One of the biggest complaints was that the application's directions were often leading users to the wrong locations—a fatal error when your only job is to provide navigation. Apple's CEO, Tim Cook, could have ignored the complaints and quietly fixed the errors, but he issued a corporate apology instead.

Fear kills more dreams than failure ever will.

People Over Profit

"At Apple, we strive to make world-class products that deliver the best experience possible to our customers. With the launch of our new Maps last week, we fell short on this commitment," Cook said. "We are extremely sorry for the frustration this has caused our customers, and we are doing everything we can to make Maps better."[8]

I'm sure issuing the embarrassing letter stung and left Cook feeling exposed to competitors, but he overcame that fear and chose to do the right thing. Now the error seems like a distant memory.

Fear of the Unknown

This form of fear is one of the most nefarious because it appeals to our organizational sensibilities. Businesses are built on forecasting, and leaders spend years learning to minimize risk and place safe bets. "You have a good thing going right now," Fear whispers at a critical juncture, "and you don't know how this decision will alter your life." But those who succeed in the modern marketplace are those who take calculated but courageous risks.

Few things in life are sadder to me than people who have failed to chase their dreams (or realize them) because they were mired in fear. If you don't learn to manage it, fear will cloud you. It will limit your vision. And your options. And your potential. No one has accomplished anything great without conquering fear and taking risks. Every leader must choose which they value more: courage or comfort.

ASSASSINATE FEAR

Adopting new practices can be scary. When I thought about launching a company with a radical set of values, I didn't know how it would work. I didn't know how the organization could survive while giving away seven dollars from every sale or paying our team members more than the industry average. If you decide to live out a revolutionary set of principles in your life and work, you'll probably get scared too. The reason the seven beliefs aren't adopted by everyone in the marketplace is because they are difficult to implement. It's called "breaking the system" because it is hard and it hurts.

But if you're a leader, a manager, an entrepreneur, take heart. You're already courageous. You already have the DNA to live this out. You have the chops to make changes. Otherwise, you'd be in the trash heap out back and not sitting in your office working overtime. You just need to release what is already inside of you.

Create space for courage.

Implement systems *now* that will allow for courageous decisions to take shape *later.* Leaders' schedules have a way of filling up quickly if they aren't guarded, so I am constantly making sure I have enough margin in my life to be bold. The temptation is to sit back, circle the wagons, protect yourself, and go on autopilot. If you aren't intentional about creating space for courage, it will not happen spontaneously. At

Sevenly, we have a budget set aside for testing new projects, and we allow employees time to dream. Do the same for yourself.

Begin planning now.

Risky decisions are not nearly as daunting when they are calculated and thought through. Seek out the advice of others who've walked similar paths, and then craft a plan to execute the vision you're cooking up. Being a courageous leader is not just about being bold but also about taking the *right kinds* of risks. Planning will help you do this.

Create a safety net.

I was so afraid when launching Sevenly, I sat down and listed every person I knew who I could turn to for a job if my start-up failed and everything fell apart. I folded up the paper with that scribbled list and placed it in the drawer of my desk so I could move forward with boldness. Even today, with millions of dollars in annual revenue, I still pull that list out after a tough day and say to myself, "If this doesn't work out, I've got ideas and options. So I might as well be brave today."

Similarly, we took in a seed investment for $125,000 when Sevenly was six months old. We chose not to use it, and stuck it in our reserve account instead. This allowed us to take some big risks early on. Maybe you need to do the same, to write down your back-up plan or construct a financial cushion. It's exponentially more dangerous to walk a tightrope without a safety net.

Invite others to join you in the fear.

The best way to fight fear is to bring someone into it with you. Fear is scarier when you face it alone. At Sevenly, whenever we are making a difficult decision, we convene a room full of others. By myself, I'd run scared. It's easier to press on when others are walking with me.

"These are the times that call for bold, confident, courageous leadership," Susan Tardanico, CEO of the Authentic Leadership Alliance, wrote in *Forbes*. "As history has shown, those with the guts to step forward, take some risks, and lead change during downturns will be the winners as the economy rebounds."[9]

Becoming a people-over-profit organization may be expensive and take time, but it is worth it. It's like hiring a mechanic to change the air filter on your car only to realize that the gaskets need cleaning, the alternator is about to die, and the manifold is on its last leg. You could keep driving the automobile for a while if you don't want to pay the price, but it is so much better when you do what you need to do to make sure everything is working properly. Courage is having the strength of character to persist and hold on to ideas in the face of opposition, fear, and high costs.

After Ray C. Anderson passed away, Interface was a transformed company living by a radical set of values and more successful than ever. They were still the largest producer of modular carpet with more than 8,000 employees. Their

If you change nothing, nothing will change.

People Over Profit

second quarter profit the year he died rose nearly 70 percent to $12.8 million.[10]

Of Anderson, the new Interface president and CEO, Dan Hendrix, said, "He had the courage to try and change the industry, and he was clearly a visionary."[11]

If Ray Anderson were here today, he would tell you that making those valiant decisions was daunting but, oh, so worth it.

So be bold. Be brave. You'll be glad you did.

PART 3

———

BREAK THE SYSTEM FOR "GOOD"

———

When I sat down to pen a previous chapter, I planned to open with a positive example from JCPenney. Then I did some digging and discovered the organization has some serious issues that need to be addressed. In 2011, for example, the company paid CEO Ron Johnson $53.3 million.[1] That's a CEO-to-worker pay gap of 1,795 to 1, a ratio the *Los Angeles Times* rightly called "obscene."[2]

JCPenney has worked to rectify this inequity, but the situation forced me to confront an important question: If an organization commits to some, but not all, of the seven beliefs, are they to be considered a people-over-profit company?

Many companies possess two or three of the aforementioned beliefs—often pursuing the easiest or most natural for them to nurture—while ignoring the others. What if a business has all the authenticity in the world but is not courageous? What if they are courageous but sell a terrible product? What if they are financially transparent but lace their advertisements with spin and weasel words?

Breaking the system means shutting it down. Ending it. Starting a revolution. To break a system, you have to overwhelm it. And this cannot be accomplished by a halfhearted or partial commitment to new behaviors. Becoming a people-over-profit company is like baking a cake. You can have the correct amount of eggs, flour, and salt, but if you don't add any sugar, no one at the party will want a slice.

On the other hand, uniting all seven beliefs has the power to break the system—not just for now, but once and for all.

A people-over-profit company must commit to *all* seven beliefs.

———

People Over Profit

It's actually possible to create a world where the Honest Era is no longer an era, but rather just the way things are. We can create a new and permanent future where people hold companies accountable, the marketplace honors those it serves, and *capitalism* is no longer a dirty word.

By adopting the seven beliefs in your personal and professional life, you have the power to create a sustainable future where the marketplace is dominated by those who are committed to telling the truth, positively impacting the world, and valuing people. The net effect is that you'll end up living with purpose, become even more successful, and achieve good that will outlive you.

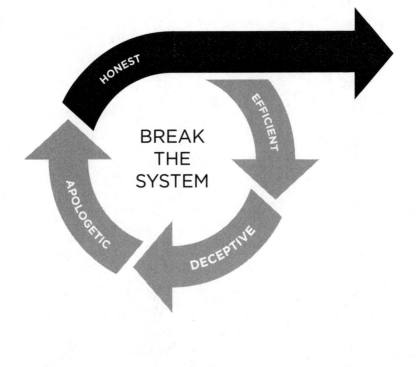

How do you begin?

First, you need to be honest about your current state. Which era is your organization, team, and household operating in? Humans are intuitive and have a sense of where they are, but answering this question will still require a little bit of investigation.

Once you understand where you are, you need to determine how to get to where you want to go. Where should you begin? Which beliefs could you and your organization adopt now? And what about your home life? These principles don't just apply to your work environment but also to your spending and social habits. How can you live what you believe after you've punched out?

And what about expectations? How long should transformation take? Organizations are made of people, and the more people you have, the slower change occurs. Change happens more quickly when you have buy-in from the top. How can you get those above you to fight alongside for better business, better behaviors, and a better system?

Transformation is possible whether you're an intern, entrepreneur, or executive. It doesn't matter if you work for a giant corporation like JCPenney or own a small boutique flower shop, have two employees or two thousand, are in charge of a multimillion dollar budget or scrounging to gather seed money.

Creating a people-over-profit world begins with you, right now, where you are.

12

LIVE "GOOD"

Who are the most powerful people in your organization? The CEO? The board of directors? The majority shareholders? Wrong. The most powerful people are your customers. These people can put you out of business or propel you to unimaginable heights. They are either your lifeblood or your lethal injection. Those who refuse to take them seriously become the authors of their own demise.

Recognizing this can leave one feeling a bit insignificant, but it is also incredibly empowering. Because you, too, are a customer. Which is to say,

You are one of the most powerful people in the marketplace.

The way you spend your money will help determine who stays in business and who goes belly up. How you talk about a company on social media with followers or over coffee with friends or at a reunion with family can dictate that organization's future. The decisions you make will help determine prices, expected levels of quality, and which products are in demand.

You may be an entrepreneur or established business leader, but you are also a consumer of hats and hamburgers, movie tickets and massages. If your boss hands you a pink slip today, you'll still be a consumer. If you decide to become a stay-at-home mom or dad, you'll still be a consumer. When you retire, you'll still be a consumer. So long as you're breathing, you'll still be a consumer.

And this means you are powerful.

In order to break the system, then, we must first learn to be good consumers. But most people are passive participants in the marketplace. They make purchases and select goods without much thought or intentionality—except maybe when it comes to price.

Think about your last trip to the grocery store. How much did you think about whether or not the products on your list utilized sustainable packaging or paid a fair wage to the farmers and manufacturers who produced it? Did you consider whether or not the company was transparent, honest, and accountable? Did you put anything in your shopping cart that was stamped with weasel words or sensational ad slogans?

Do what you can, with what you have, where you are.

—

Theodore Roosevelt

Most consumers engage in blind purchasing or naive purchasing or robotic purchasing. Few engage in intentional and informed shopping that values and promotes a set of beliefs or standards.

What if you demanded uncompromising quality in every item you bought, even if it cost you a bit more? What if you chose between two comparable products based on which company was more charitable and generous? What if you opted for products of companies that treated their employees well and had a reasonable CEO-to-worker pay ratio? And what if you told everyone you knew to follow suit? How might those decisions change the marketplace?

ACTIONS SPEAK

In order to create a people-over-profit world, we need to become intentional consumers by taking the good approach.

Buying Good

The average American household spends more than $50,000 per year in the marketplace.[1] That's a heap of moolah, which is to say, a lot of power. To create a better world, you need to invest in products and services that align with your values and beliefs. Become a skeptical shopper. Read labels. Investigate the ingredients you can't pronounce. And remember that even if it is a good product, it doesn't mean it is a great company. Don't fall for empty marketing ploys. Be cautious of companies that overuse unregulated phrases like "all natural." Research some of the organizations you patronize, and list out your priorities and nonnegotiables for those you support.

This isn't always easy to do, especially if you live in a rural community or are on a fixed income. A few years ago, I moved with my wife, Veronica, to the mountains, where we have limited options. But every opportunity we have, we take. Sure, it might be more expensive. But integrity often costs money. And being healthy does too. We've had to cut back in other areas in order to buy better goods from better companies. From deodorant to toothpaste to produce to cleaning products, we try to support accountable companies committed to the seven beliefs. Here's the kicker: the products are almost always better. So we're satisfied with the decisions we've made and the sacrifices that made them possible.

Luckily, there is a recent trend—particularly among millennials—to leverage their marketplace influence for good. In 2012, 47 percent of consumers said that every month they purchase at least one brand that supports a good cause. (That's nearly a 50 percent increase from 2010.)[2] But what if this 47 percent became 97 percent? And what if those standards were applied to everything they bought?

You're beginning to see the big picture? The way you spend your money matters.

Giving Good

Your charitable donations are just as important as your spending decisions. But be advised: if you aren't proactive, you will not give. A close friend of mine sets aside 20 percent of his money into a special account each month. He doesn't know exactly where it is going to go when he makes the deposit, but it grants him the ability to give when needs arise. The account is used for donations to churches and charities, helping down-and-out friends, and random acts of kindness.

And giving isn't just a financial reality. How intentional are you about budgeting your time and talents? Just as one might set aside a percentage of his or her income for charitable donations, I have an invisible account where I store up an amount of hours for donating my gifts and time to organizations that promote good. I donate a chunk of my time every month, for example, to speak and write and volunteer for free. You can't do everything for everyone, so take a minute to write down which organizations and charities really get you excited. Then give time and talent in that direction.

Sharing Good

Seventy-two percent of consumers now say they would recommend a brand that supports a good cause.[3] Are you one of them? One of the biggest drivers of money in the market is the mouth. According to Nielsen, word of mouth is still the most trusted resource for marketplace recommendations.[4] How are you using your voice to nurture the seven people-over-profit beliefs and companies that adhere to them?

Take time to phone friends who consume the same items and make recommendations. Register with review sites and applications such as Yelp, Foursquare, and Urbanspoon. Increasing social voice will increase return on investment and drive online search engine activity.[5]

IF OTHERS KNEW AS YOU KNEW, THEY WOULD DO AS YOU DO.

Are you artistic? Produce a documentary about an industry that is failing the marketplace or creating exceptional products. Are you connected on social media? Tweet about good brands and organizations. Are you a blogger? When you find something wrong or uncover something laudable, share it with your readers.

Word of mouth is not dead. But it will be if "we the people" stop talking. We must leverage our networks and voices to expose the bad and amplify the good in society. As I like to say, if others knew as you knew, they would do as you do. But they won't know it if you don't show it.

My dream is to move my family to Bend, Oregon—a place where there is less noise and less crowding and less distraction. It's a place that seems ideal for the human body to exist. I'm not a super-hippie crazy person, but I long for a more natural existence. My wife and I plan to grow much of our food and raise some animals and generate some electricity and produce many of the products we now buy.

But even if we get partially off the grid, we'll still be powerful consumers. We'll still have to buy mattresses and air conditioning units and gasoline. We'll still have cell phones and computers. We'll still eat out on occasion. We've committed to never forget that we are, and always will be, some of the most powerful people in the marketplace. And you are too. No matter how much money you make or where you live.

So go ahead and live "good."

Your world will be better because of it.

13

LAUNCH "GOOD"

When people first discover a better way to do business and an improved way to live, it often transforms them into a starter. The desire to launch a company or club or nonprofit smokes inside of them as the spark for a better world catches fire and begins to blaze. No wonder entrepreneurship is considered one of the biggest trends in the twenty-first-century marketplace.

"At a time when the world seems to be cracking into ever more smaller groups demanding their rights, when global warming is a debated threat, when violence seems to be on a forward march, entrepreneurship offers an antidote," wrote Steve Strauss for *USA Today*. "Entrepreneurship is about creating something, not destroying anything. It is about using creativity and teamwork and intelligence to solve problems. It forges bonds and moves us forward."[1]

There is often an increase in entrepreneurs following a recession because capable people have lost their jobs and have to figure out a way to make money. Rather than find another nine-to-five working for "the man," they dream of paving their own paths. They imagine what it might look like to conduct business without the most common defective behaviors in their industry. If the desire marinates long enough, they attempt to launch better organizations—ones that right the wrongs of the companies that failed them.

Few moments over the last century have been as well primed for launching new ventures as this one. The United States just came out of a massive recession. Consumer confidence and trust in corporate darlings are flailing. The market is hungry for alternatives. People are open to trying new solutions built on fresh ideas. The digital age and the rise of social media have leveled the playing field, where a scrappy business with a loyal fan base can grab market exposure on par with corporate giants and their multimillion-dollar advertising revenue.

The trend in entrepreneurship is coinciding with a trend in social responsibility. Businesses feel increasing pressure to have a "cause component" associated with their products and services. Major colleges around the country—including Northwestern University, Stanford University, and Baylor University—are launching courses, concentrations, and majors in social entrepreneurship and corporate responsibility.

I believe we are on the cusp of a new era, when every organization is expected to contribute to a better world. Gone are the days of launching companies that are only good for corporate tycoons and not for society. I envision a world where a dad buys his son a toy and the child asks, "Dad, what good does buying this toy accomplish? What causes does it support?" I believe we are approaching a moment where most of the products in the marketplace are improving the world in some way, and those that don't, look stupid, feel out of place, aren't trusted, and risk being marginalized.

AT A BASIC LEVEL, THERE ARE NO BAD COMPANIES—JUST BAD LEADERS.

"Your business doesn't even attempt to contribute to society," a customer might say. "Why aren't you accomplishing good? You need to get in line or get out of the marketplace."

We've begun transitioning from old capitalism, where the market was focused on creating a satisfactory solution to problems and making as much money from it as possible, to new capitalism, where the market seeks to pursue a mission, accomplish social good, and as a result, make money. The Western economic system has gotten a bad rap, but the real problem is not capitalism; it is irresponsible capitalists who take advantage of the system and abuse the public's trust. At a basic level, there are no bad companies—just bad leaders.

Capitalism is good. When its leaders are caring. When its leaders are compassionate. When its leaders measure more than just profit at the bottom line.

Stop complaining. Start creating.

People Over Profit

Starters who are committed to launching good are critical to realizing this new world. You may be launching an Etsy shop with hand-knitted beanies sold in a one-for-one model or making better-quality kitchen tables from reclaimed wood in your spare time. You may be launching an initiative to organize garage sales throughout your city that donate profits to an anti-sex-trafficking organization or creating a business that sells custom jewelry without the obscene markups that are common in the marketplace. Regardless, you need to launch well and launch right.

SMASH THE GAS PEDAL, BUT WEAR YOUR SEATBELT

As a starter myself, I know the urges and compulsions to do better business. I've tested which processes work and which ones can kill you. Additionally, I've studied dozens of start-ups that operate on the seven beliefs. From their experiences and mine, here are four tips for how to launch good.

1. Start now.

Once entrepreneurs determine *what* they want to do, they often get stuck in the *how* phase. How does one create a web presence, find affordable vendors, create a workable supply chain, register for a business license, file corporate taxes, and all the rest? The uncertainty and complexity of these questions can stall the process of starting. This was the inspiration of my newest venture StartupCamp.com,

STARTERS BITE OFF MORE THAN THEY CAN CHEW IN HOPES THEY CAN QUICKLY LEARN TO CHEW IT.

———

an educational membership for aspiring entrepreneurs, bloggers, and dreamers.

Over the past years, I watched the best entrepreneurs—in fact, every one I've ever met—learn by doing and not by learning to do. They don't wait until they get a PhD in their field or until they have read every cornerstone business text or have mountains of cash stored up in their savings accounts. They just jump into the deep end of the pool, use the skills and knowledge they have, and paddle like crazy. Starters bite off more than they can chew in hopes they can quickly learn to chew it.

If you're stuck in the *how* phase and need a permission slip to move forward, consider this it. When you sense fear of the unknown, it's often a sign you need to walk into, not away from, what is repelling you. Fear is the exact opposite of what you want your life to be. Whether it is starting a charity or pursuing a goal or asking a girl out or starting a business, fear leads you away from your desires. So turn around, risk bravely, take the plunge, and start now.

2. Start right.

One of the worst words an entrepreneur can let creep into his or her vocabulary is *eventually*. Though there may be a noble impetus for starting a new venture, the starter is tempted to compromise these core commitments early on. Don't believe the lie that you will do "good" later when you

See the fear and do it anyway.

—

People Over Profit

#PeopleOverProfit

have enough profit or margin or exposure. You won't. As with generosity, it must be built in and not tacked on. So start right and launch the organization *now* as you would want it to be *eventually*.

3. Start proud.

The good components of your new venture should be situated front and center. Don't hide or tuck these away. Put them on the front of everything. If you spend more to manufacture a good locally, why wouldn't you share that with boldness? If you use recycled content, why wouldn't you print a symbol denoting that on your packaging? If you donate a percentage of your profits to a good cause, why wouldn't you want to let your customers know?

Grab your bullhorn and shout, don't whisper. Make such a commotion that those who aren't accomplishing good will shake in their boots. The good component of your organization is not an accent pillow on the couch in the parlor; it's the bright-red front door in the center of your house.

4. Don't stop starting.

One characteristic I've noticed among the most transcendent established companies is that they perpetually act like start-ups. A great example is the fast-food company Chick-fil-A. Their corporate politics aside, this chicken sandwich icon has one of the most loyal customer bases in the American marketplace. And they've built and sustained it by retaining a start-up mentality. Chick-fil-A is constantly giving away free sandwiches—to businesses and nonprofits, in raffles and radio giveaways. If you're one of the first customers to dine at a new store, Chick-fil-A will even give you a year's supply of free chicken sandwiches. McDonald's doesn't do that. But a new business is always giving away free product to get the word out.

Another start-up–style aspect common among transcendent companies is a bent toward collaboration rather than competition. Capitalism has told us that we shouldn't partner with anyone, that everything is proprietary, and that anyone who isn't on our team is our enemy. There's a reason that the head of a similar company to mine wrote the foreword to this book. We don't think we're competing; we're on the same team.

Transcendent companies also resist an elitist mentality, maintaining the humble posture of start-ups. Whole Foods, for example, is constantly looking for new partnerships with scrappy small vendors and is willing to carry unknown brands. Rather than cozying up to corporate giants and operating on an elitist mentality, they opt for local flair and make each location feel like it is *your* Whole Foods. Though they are big, they are still small. You, too, should commit to never outgrow being a passionate, principled start-up.

If you feel called to launch something, congratulations. It's beautiful when your work is not just work, but actually a purpose. It makes your life better and your friendships better and creates a natural extension of what you already love. A good company is so much more than a job, especially when you were the one who birthed it. So I'm tipping my hat to you, my fellow starters. By launching now, right, proud, and perpetually, you're helping create a better world. But you're also building a better you.

14

LEAD "GOOD"

Once you determine that you want to live and work in a people-over-profit mindset, one question becomes paramount: "Do I feel called to stay or to start?" Only you can answer this, and it will take some serious reflection, prayer, and conversations with friends, family, and mentors.

If you feel called to start, know that you may have chosen an easier path. Yes, you read that correctly. People often assume that entrepreneurs are gutsy, but those who feel called to stay and change from within are sometimes the most courageous. It's easier to keep a baby healthy from birth than it is to cure an elderly person with cancer. In the same way, it is easier to start a better organization and remain better than to take one that is firmly entrenched in bad habits and turn the tide. Swimming upstream in an organization that has been flowing fast and fierce in the opposite direction for decades or longer requires moxie.

So if you work for an established business that seems stuck in the Efficient or Deceptive Eras, don't—I repeat, don't—quit your job. First determine if you feel called to stay. We need carefully placed operatives inside juggernaut corporations to help change those organizations from within.

If that's you, and you feel called to stay planted where you are and become a change agent from inside the belly of a corporate beast, I want to offer you fair warning. There will be days when the mounting resistance from coworkers and bosses will make you feel like you're banging your head against the wall. The experience may be emotionally draining and might even place your job in jeopardy. You've chosen the right, albeit more difficult, path for yourself. But the effect, if you play your cards right, can be earth-shattering.

If you don't believe me, just ask Hannah Jones. She is vice president of sustainable business and innovation for Nike. When Jones joined the company in 1998, few people were using the words *sustainable* and *Nike* in the same sentence. The company was experiencing an onslaught of global criticism for social injustices linked to their manufacturing and supply-chain practices.

Prior to working at Nike, Jones had worked at the BBC on social action campaigns and for an NGO as an advocate on issues such as AIDS/HIV and racism. It would have been easier for her to have remained in companies that were sympathetic to her passions rather than taking a job that would most assuredly paint a giant target on her back. But Jones took the job working for Nike in a division that was then called "Corporate Responsibility."[1]

Jones began to open channels of communication with Nike's critics, as well as academics and nonprofits who could help the organization brainstorm improvements. They began addressing everything from workers' rights to sustainable materials to eliminating toxic chemicals used in screen printing.

"The first counterintuitive moment (CM) was when we embraced transparency," she says. "Our next CM came when we said 'guess what, we're also going to be accountable.' In 2006, we released our factory locations marking the first time this was ever done in our industry. This moment also marked us taking a non-competitive business risk that changed the system."[2]

Sustainability . . .

Transparency . . .

Accountability . . .

Honoring workers . . .

Changing the system . . .

Any of this starting to sound familiar?

Today, Hannah Jones leads a team of 140 people devoted to sustainability at the largest seller of athletic footwear and apparel in the world. The company now releases a corporate responsibility report and launched Nikebetterworld.com so that consumers can track their efforts to improve corporate practices. Under her watch, Nike has gone from being one of the worst corporate perpetrators of social injustices to being praised as a leader in sustainability.

Nike still has room to grow, but none of this progress would have been possible had she not decided to lead good from *inside* an organization failing to operate as a people-over-profit organization by almost every data point.

If you think you might be the Hannah Jones of your organization, here's how to get started.

THE ART OF WAR

Remember, you're not fighting a common cold; this is cancer. People are going to push back against you pushing back against them. You'll need to be methodical and calculating, often trying multiple curatives until you find one that works. Sometimes you'll need to push the host to the brink of death in order to save it.

Craft a plan of attack.

Any plan is better than no plan, and a well-mapped-out plan is better than one that is thrown together. The more thorough your plan of attack, the higher the chance of success.

OFFER TO TAKE A PAY CUT SO AN UNDERPAID EMPLOYEE BELOW YOU CAN GET A RAISE.

The first step in any attack plan is to live it out yourself. People need to see it before they believe it. Model the things you believe for those who report to you, work beside you, and lead you. Are you advocating for a companywide recycling program? Bring a blue recycling trash can to collect paper, glass, and aluminum from around the office and take it home with you at the end of the day. Are you an upper-level manager advocating for a more equitable CEO-to-worker pay ratio? Offer to take a pay cut so an underpaid employee below you can get a raise.

Consider who your allies might be and how you could form alliances with them. You can't do this alone, so meet with them regularly. Also determine who your foes are and where you're likely to encounter obstacles. Think about how to circumvent or avoid these stumbling blocks.

Once you've drafted a plan, remain flexible. No plan comes off exactly as you hope. You'll almost certainly need to make adjustments along the way.

Charge ahead slowly.

You need specific and measurable goals if you're going to transform your organization into a people-over-profit business. One of the biggest misconceptions among internal

He who fails to plan, plans to fail.

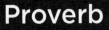

Proverb

change makers—what we might call "intrapreneurs"—is that goals need to be dramatic. But change doesn't have to come with the sunrise, and it mustn't happen all at once.

Intrapreneurs often want to shoot for the stars and land on the moon. But in their desire to change the world, they can miss profound opportunities for changing a single process or policy or life. The people-over-profit challenge is to begin slowly adopting the seven beliefs, building steadily like a bricklayer. Each month or quarter or year, you lay a brick or two. Always building, but sometimes slowly.

Maybe this year you'll demand ethical manufacturing practices. Next year, perhaps you'll begin paying people a fair wage or increasing quality where it is lacking. After that, you might begin finding ways to become more transparent and accountable with corporate finances. This will require a daily dose of bravery and discipline, but step-by-step, progress will come.

Be willing to die.

Are you ready to lose friends, encounter resistance, and even forfeit your job? If so, you're ready to move forward. Transformation requires boldness. So when you see an opportunity for change, take it. Don't be afraid to request a meeting with the CEO or even the senior vice president of your department. Also, keep records of everything you've done in case you are terminated. That way, you can prove to others that you were only attempting to make the company better and more successful, which is every good employee's ultimate goal.

At the same time, you'll need a heavy dose of emotional maturity to move forward. Know when to hold your tongue and when to stop pushing. Learn to empathize with others' positions rather than becoming judgmental. Some of the greatest leaders throughout history possessed a rare mix of strength and meekness.

Leading good is a difficult and dangerous road to travel. It's fraught with potholes and detours and bandits who wish to harm you. It stretches on forever, even after your time comes to an end. But if you can successfully traverse it, the world will be better for it.

15

EVEN "GOOD" CAN GO BAD

On April 8, 2014, I was terminated from Sevenly.

Sitting at El Torito restaurant, two investors, who we had brought on board only a handful of months prior, told me they were taking the company in a different direction. I was not a critical part of the leadership structure in this new vision. Strong words were used, and in my opinion, the decision and the way it was handled came from a "profit over people" mindset. The change was effective immediately, and plans were already in place to inform the Sevenly team later that day.

Shock.

Disbelief.

Hurt.

I wanted to slip away and throw up. Or weep. Or scream. But none of these things would make a difference. As an owner of less than 51 percent, I was helpless. The decision had been made.

Untold numbers of people have found themselves sitting in the same seat, and perhaps you're one of them. You gave a portion of your life's prime to something you love. You made sacrifices for it. You bled and sweat and cried buckets of tears for it. Countless late nights and early mornings were donated to the cause. But in a blink, it all disappears. Like dry sand, it slips through your fingers. The only thing left is residue, mere memories of what once was.

As it turns out, even "good" can go bad.

By this, I don't mean that Sevenly somehow became a bad company that was no longer committed to our founding beliefs and principles. Rather, I mean that even the best companies can disappoint you personally. They can change and grow and mature, and over time, cease to be a good fit for you. A season may roll in, like a lightning-fast winter, and you find yourself a mismatch. The music may even stop, and you find out that you don't have a chair anymore.

What should you do in such a moment? How should you respond?

There isn't a set of tidy tips or simple ways to face this kind of adversity perfectly. Sometimes there's not enough juice in life's lemons to make lemonade. And even if you respond right, there is no promise that it will all work out in the end. But looking back, there are several important lessons that I believe can help entrepreneurs and employees prepare for and respond to such a situation:

1. Pick partners wisely.

Those who help you carry out your organization's mission are almost as important as the mission itself. Think before you take on investors, and consider every hire carefully, no matter how "insignificant" you think the position might be. The team around you is critical, and they will help chart your future. And remember, just because they are great people doesn't mean they are the *right* great people.

2. You be you.

One of the biggest lies that business leaders and entrepreneurs can tell themselves is, "I am what I do." In the wake of this conversation, I became acutely aware that I had failed to fully differentiate my identity from my company's. I was Sevenly and Sevenly was me. The DNA of the company and my own genetic material were one and the same. As a result, my job title wasn't the only thing affected by this news. My identity also took a hit.

So you be you and not what you do. Always remember that your identity is not your job title or list of professional accomplishments. This will help you be a healthier leader and respond to changes with maturity and levelheadedness.

3. Own your failures.

Anytime you encounter a disappointment in life, the tendency is to blame others. But every pancake has two sides, as does every story. When others fail you, rest assured you've also failed them. Professional crisis is a great opportunity for personal reflection. *What mistakes did I make? Where could I have done a better job? What needs improvement in my life?*

I realize when looking back on my time leading Sevenly that I was often a deeply flawed leader. I made tactical failures, surrounding myself with gifted people but not always the *right* people. I made the company too much about me, and sometimes that blinded me to the big picture. I was too aggressive in moments when I should have been more passive, and too passive on matters where I should have been more aggressive. I've made commitments to improve in each of these areas.

Many leaders have found themselves in similar situations to mine—Donald Trump, Martha Stewart, Steve Jobs—but they let the experience propel them to even greater heights. Disappointment can be either destructive or instructive. You get to choose which.

How people treat you is their story; how you react is yours.

—

Wayne Dyer

4. Learn to let go.

One of the most difficult tasks in life is walking away from something you love. But as Kenny Rogers might have said back in his Gambler days, you have to know when to fold 'em and walk away from the table. Life often comes in seasons, and you don't want to be caught standing in a snowstorm wearing Bermuda shorts. You should love your work, but don't fall in love with it. You should enjoy your work, but don't grow obsessed with it.

Always be prepared to let go of it if you need to, and always be prepared for the next season.

5. Let yourself grieve.

When there is change, there is loss. If your company dies or decides to live without you, a grieving process is not just warranted, but necessary. One of the reasons that soldiers returning from war suffer from PTSD is because they don't grieve the experiences of the battlefield. Don't stuff away the emotions you're feeling. Let them out, but only in an appropriate manner. I spent countless hours crying after receiving the news, but I'd rather over-grieve and move on too late than under-grieve and move on a day too soon.

Remember that part of grieving is forgiveness. And you have to forgive those you think have done you wrong, even if they don't agree with you or ask for it. Forgive those who have failed you, even if they're not sorry.

6. Put the torch down.

If you've been hurt, you'll want to hurt others back. When there is pain, there is anger. When there is confusion, there is anger. When there is loss, there is anger. And anger can be one of the most destructive emotions if left unchecked. Because if anger sits, anger sours. And when anger sours, it ferments into hatred and bitterness, which like acid, destroys the containers in which they are stored.

Resist the urge to burn bridges. Put down the torch and lower your pitchfork. Relationships are important, and the ones you don't think you'll ever need again you often do. Value those who've made you angry as highly as you wish they had valued you.

At the end of the day, people still matter. Those you've left behind matter. Those you think may have wronged you matter. The good people they still serve matter. And nothing will test whether or not you truly believe this like having something "good" feel as if it has gone bad for you.

Each morning when I rise and slip on a Sevenly shirt, I swell with pride, not bitterness. Though I am no longer the company's CEO, I will always be its founder, and at this time, still a proud part-owner. They are still a great company with great people and a great mission and great products, and they still accomplish the impossible—giving millions of dollars to worthy causes.

Bitterness is like drinking rat poison and waiting for the rat to die.

—

Anne Lamott

I choose to focus on what we accomplished from Sevenly's inception to my final day on payroll. I choose resilience and hope and positivity. Because the marketplace viability of the seven beliefs—ideas that Sevenly still embraces—holds true regardless of circumstances.

People *still* matter more than profit.

And they always will.

+

WHY THIS BOOK IS SO SHORT

There's nothing worse than finishing a book and thinking, *Dang, I got the author's basic idea in the first few chapters. Why did they force me to read 200 pages of reiterations and redundancies?*

Unfortunately that is not an uncommon experience, because when it comes to books, higher page count equals higher price point, which equals higher profit. Too many authors bloat their content in an effort to stretch an "article-length idea" into a book or transform a short book into a long book. In this way, many books are the ultimate profit-over-people product.

I think this disrespects you, the reader.

The work you hold in your hands is a little more than thirty thousand words, including the foreword and this note. That's about half the length of similar books in the marketplace. It is, by many accounts, "too short" to be a traditional business book. The heck with that. When I sat down to pen *People Over Profit*, I purposed to make it as lean and concise as possible. I made a commitment to avoid rambling when I could speak directly, to resist the temptation to conform to industry standards by adding unnecessary content. Why?

Because I believe that people matter.

Because I believe you matter.

Because I believe your time matters.

You're welcome!

CHALLENGE: TAKING THE NEXT STEP

I'm proud to say I've read more than 200 books in my life. And like many of you, I've only finished about half of them. For those of you who made it to the end, who believe in this movement, and who are ready to turn the information into transformation, I have created a short, yet comprehensive study guide.

This workbook will walk with you on your journey to value people over profit. Inside, I ask the hard questions and help you form the external strategies you can implement into your business. This guide is great for groups, executive teams, and entrepreneurs alike. Together, we will rip away the old and learn to value honesty over deception, transparency over secrecy, authenticity over hype, and, ultimately, people over profit.

Learn more at PeopleOverProfit.com/Study-Guide.

ACKNOWLEDGMENTS

Jesus

I'm humbled by your grace. Thank you for choosing me.

Veronica

Thank you for loving me no matter what.

Aria

You have given me a great reason to live, grow, and thrive.

Dad

Thank you for supporting my entrepreneurship. You believed in me when others didn't.

Mom

Thank you for loving me as a child. It's surely helped me develop into the man I am today.

Carol

Your consistency has been a healing hand in our family and my story. Thank you.

Johnny and Cindy

Thank you for being there for us. You've raised an incredible daughter and supporter.

Matthew

Your story has inspired me. Our future will be bright, together.

Aaron and Jen

Your unconditional love has been at the center of the hard times we've had. Your friendship is incredible. Thank you.

Amanda

I don't know what I would do without you. Thank you for sticking by me through thick and thin.

Brady

Your endless support will never be forgotten. Thank you.

Jonathan

Your help with this manuscript was astonishing. I will not forget it.

Chris

Thank you for seeing my potential.

Chad

Your hard work on this project has been nothing but impressive.

Daniel

Thank you for taking a risk on me. Your support will not be forgotten

Jon

Your friendship has been deeper than most. Thank you for seeing what most miss.

TK

This dream would not be possible without you. I finally realize it.

Jim

Your heart of restoration has healed a hard story. Thank you for the undying efforts.

Aaron C.

Your partnership was a story I will never forget. We did it.

ABOUT THE AUTHOR

Dale Partridge is a social entrepreneur and founder of Sevenly.org and StartupCamp.com. Described as "a mind who feels the trends before market," Partridge teaches leaders and organizations how to position their brand, love their people, and develop profitable corporate social responsibility programs.

He's a renowned expert on branding, consumer psychology, and marketplace trends. He is an avid speaker and has been featured in various business publications and on national networks, including on the cover of *Entrepreneur Magazine*, Fox News, NBC, *Inc.* magazine, Mashable, MSN Money, *Forbes*, and the *Los Angeles Times*. Dale lives with his family in Bend, Oregon.

Twitter and Instagram: @DalePartridge
E-mail: Dale@PeopleOverProfit.com
www.DalePartridge.com

NOTES

Chapter 0

1. Bill Hardekopf, "Consumers Paid $32 Billion in Overdraft Fees In 2012," *Forbes Online*, April 2, 2013, http://www.forbes.com/sites/moneybuilder/2013/04/02/consumers-paid-32-billion-in-overdraft-fees-in-2012/.
2. Edelman/StrategyOne, "Goodpurpose Study, Executive Summary" (New York: Edelman, 2012), 2.
3. National Center for Charitable Statistics, "Quick Facts About Nonprofits," Urban Institute website, 2013, http://nccs.urban.org/statistics/quickfacts.cfm; Ibid., "Frequently Asked Questions," http://nccs.urban.org/faq/.

The Cycle We're Stuck In

1. William Strauss and Neil Howe, *The Fourth Turning* (New York: Broadway Books, 1998), [[INSERT PAGE NUMBER]].

2. Mark Twain, quoted in Strauss and Howe, *The Fourth Turning*, 11.

3. This Day in History, "May 1, 1926: Ford Factory Workers Get 40-Hour Week," History Channel, http://www.history.com/this-day-in-history/ford-factory-workers-get-40-hour-week.

4. "The 50 Worst Cars of All Time," *Time*, 2007, http://content.time.com/time/specials/2007/article/0,28804,1658545_1658498_1657866,00.html; Mark Dowie, "Pinto Madness," *Mother Jones*, September/October 1977, http://www.motherjones.com/politics/1977/09/pinto-madness?page=1.

Chapter 1

1. "Our 3 Basic Beliefs," Walmart website, accessed August 5, 2014, http://ethics.walmartstores.com/StatementOfEthics/BasicBeliefs.aspx.

2. "Sam Walton Biography," Biography.com, accessed August 5, 2014, http://www.biography.com/people/sam-walton-9523270.

3. Owen Thomas, "Airbnb Could Soon Do $1 Billion a Year in Revenues," *Business Insider*, January 24, 2013, http://www.businessinsider.com/airbnb-billion-revenues-2013-1; Caleb Melby, "Who Will Get Rich from Sky High Airbnb Valuation?" *Forbes*, October 19, 2012, http://www.forbes.com/sites/calebmelby/2012/10/19/peter-thiel-may-invest-150-million-in-airbnb-at-2-5-billion-valuation/; Natalie Waterworth, "Company Review: Airbnb," *Talented Heads*, June 14, 2013, http://www.talentedheads.com/2013/06/14/company-review-airbnb/.

4. "America's Most-Hated Companies: The Very Bottom Line," *The Economist*, December 20, 2005, http://www.economist.com/node/5323688; Douglas A. McIntyre and Michael Be Sauter, "5 Most-Hated Companies in America," MSN Money, January 14, 2013,

http://money.msn.com/top-stocks/c_galleryregular.
aspx?cp-documentid=250409752.

Chapter 2

1. http://www.tysonfoods.com/Our-Story/Heritage.aspx, accessed March 1, 2014.
2. Patrick Lencioni, "The Enemy of Innovation and Creativity," *The Table Group* (blog), October 2009, https://www. tablegroup.com/pat/povs/pov/?id=30.
3. Brent E. Riffel, "Tyson Foods, Inc.," The Encyclopedia of Arkansas History & Culture, last updated February 19, 2014, http://www.encyclopediaofarkansas.net/encyclopedia/entry-detail.aspx?entryID=2101.
4. David Vinjamuri, "Tyson Foods and Piglet Abuse: Is Ethical Behavior Profitable?" *Forbes*, May 11, 2012, http:// www.forbes.com/sites/davidvinjamuri/2012/05/11/ tyson-foods-and-piglet-abuse-is-ethical-behavior-profitable/.
5. Tim Worstall, "Of Course WalMart Destroys Retail Jobs: That's The Darn Point of It All," *Forbes*, March 31, 2013, http://www.forbes.com/sites/timworstall/2013/03/31/ of-course-walmart-destroys-retail-jobs-thats-the-darn-point-of-it-all/.
6. Christopher Mims, "Google's '20% Time,' Which Brought You Gmail and AdSense, Is Now as Good As Dead," *Quartz*, August 16, 2013, http://qz.com/115831/ googles-20-time-which-brought-you-gmail-and-adsense-is-now-as-good-as-dead/.
7. Jim Collins, *How the Mighty Fall: And Why Some Companies Never Give In* (New York: Collins Business Essentials, 2009), [[PAGE NUMBER]].

Chapter 3

1. Eliot Blair Smith, "'Race to Bottom' at Moody's S&P Secured

Subprime's Boom, Bust," Bloomberg.com, September 25, 2008, http://www.bloomberg.com/apps/news?pid=new sarchive&sid=ax3vfya_Vtdo; see also Eliot Blair Smith, "Bringing Down Wall Street As Ratings Let Loose Subprime Scourge," Bloomberg.com, September 24, 2008, http://www. bloomberg.com/apps/news?pid=newsarchive&sid=ah839IW TLP9s.

2. Derek Thompson, "What's Behind the Huge (and Growing) CEO-Worker Pay Gap?" *The Atlantic*, April 30, 2013, http:// www.theatlantic.com/business/archive/2013/04/whats-behind-the-huge-and-growing-ceo-worker-pay-gap/275435/.

3. Jim Collins, *How the Mighty Fall: And Why Some Companies Never Give In* (New York: Collins Business Essentials, 2009), 81.

4. Christina Romer, "Spurious Volatility in Historical Unemployment Data," *Journal of Political Economy* 94, no. 1 (1986): 1–37.

5. David M. Kennedy, *Freedom From Fear* (New York: Oxford University Press, 1999), 366.

6. Cornelia J. Strawser, ed., and Mary Meghan Ryan, *Business Statistics of the United States 2012: Patterns of Economic Change* (Lanham, MD: Rowman & Littlefield 2012), xxvi.

7. Peter S. Goodman, "U.S. Unemployment Rate Hits 10.2%, Highest in 26 Years," *New York Times*, posted November 6, 2009, http://www.nytimes.com/2009/11/07/business/economy/07jobs.html?_r=0.

Chapter 4

1. Paul Farhi, "Behind Domino's Mea Culpa Ad Campaign," *Washington Post*, posted January 13, 2010, http://www. washingtonpost.com/wp-dyn/content/article/2010/01/12/AR2010011201696.html.

2. "About Domino's Pizza: History," Dominos Pizza website, accessed August 5, 2014, http://www.dominosbiz.com/

Biz-Public-EN/Site+Content/Secondary/About+Dominos/
History/.

3. Ibid.

4. "Domino's: Customers Told Us Our Pizza Was Bad,"
Bloomberg TV (video), accessed August 5, 2014, http://
www.bloomberg.com/video/dominos-customers-told-us-our-
pizza-was-bad-4yJwqlBPROiEA2dEO67GSA.html.

5. "The Pizza Turnaround Documentary," Pizzaturnaround.com
(video), accessed August 5, 2014, http://pizzaturnaround.
com.

6. Stuart Elliott, "'Bad' Pizza Is Subject of New Domino's Spot,"
New York Times, August 27, 2010, http://mediadecoder.
blogs.nytimes.com/2010/08/27/bad-pizza-is-subject-of-new-
dominos-spot/?_php=true&_type=blogs&_r=0.

7. "Domino's: Customers Told Us Our Pizza Was Bad,"
Bloomberg TV (video).

8. Kevin Krolicki, "GM Says It 'Disappointed' and
'Betrayed' Consumers," *Reuters*, December 8, 2008,
http://www.reuters.com/article/2008/12/08/
us-gm-ad-idUSTRE4B738W20081208.

9. Belinda Luscombe, "GM's New Ad Campaign: Will It Restart
the Engines?" *Time*, June 11, 2009, http://content.time.com/
time/business/article/0,8599,1903780,00.html.

10. Steve Pendlebury, "Toyota Joins Apology Ad Parade
with 'Commitment' Commercial," *AOL News*, February
9, 2010, http://www.aolnews.com/2010/02/09/
toyota-joins-apology-ad-parade-with-commitment/.

11. "American Airlines: The New American Is Arriving,"
American Airlines website, accessed August 5, 2014, http://
www.aa.com/newamerican.

12. Jim Collins, *How the Mighty Fall: And Why Some Companies
Never Give In* (New York: Collins Business Essentials, 2009),
[[ADD PG NUMBER]].

Chapter 5

1. Lauren Drell, "6 Companies with Awesome Employee Perks," *Mashable*, August 7, 2011, http://mashable.com/2011/08/07/startup-employee-perks/.
2. Stacy Conradt, "11 of the Best Customer Service Stories Ever," last updated July 15, 2014, http://mentalfloss.com/article/30198/11-best-customer-service-stories-ever.
3. Ibid.
4. Apolis Global website, accessed August 5, 2014, http://www.apolisglobal.com/global-marketplace.

Chapter 6

1. Tatiana Morales, "From 2004: 'Super Size Me,'" *CBS News*, May 6, 2004, http://www.cbsnews.com/news/from-2004-super-size-me/.
2. Alice Van Housen, "Here's a Radical Idea—Tell the Truth!" *Fast Company*, August/September 1997, http://www.fastcompany.com/32566/heres-radical-idea-tell-truth.
3. Ibid.
4. Dodai Stewart, "'Honest' Version of Coca Cola's Anti-Obesity Ad Is Actually a Scary Truth Bomb," Jezebel, January 17, 2013, http://jezebel.com/5976720/honest-version-of-coca-colas-anti+obesity-ad-is-actually-a-scary-truth-bomb.
5. Better Business Bureau website, accessed August 5, 2014, http://memphis.bbb.org/article/its-to-everyones-benefit-to-promote-truthful-advertising-32606.
6. Sue Unerman and Jonathan Salem Baskin, *Tell the Truth: Honesty Is Your Most Powerful Marketing Tool* (Dallas: BenBella Books, 2012).
7. Martin Evans, "Honesty Test: Lack of Integrity Is Bad for the Economy, Scientists Conclude," *Telegraph*, January 25, 2012, http://www.telegraph.co.uk/news/9038164/

Honesty-test-lack-of-integrity-is-bad-for-the-economy-scientists-conclude.html.

Chapter 7

1. Jeff Hayden, "Inside a Completely Transparent Company," *Inc.*, last updated April 22, 2013, http://www.inc.com/jeff-haden/inside-buffer-company-complete-transparency.html.
2. Ibid.
3. "Timberland Responsibility," Timberland website, accessed August 5, 2014, http://responsibility.timberland.com/factories/?story=1.
4. John Hall, "10 Leaders Who Aren't Afraid to Be Transparent," *Forbes*, August 27, 2012, http://www.forbes.com/sites/johnhall/2012/08/27/10-leaders-who-arent-afraid-to-be-transparent/.
5. Meg Whitman, "The Power of Transparent Communication," Linkedin, April 23, 2013, http://www.linkedin.com/today/post/article/20130423170055-71744402-the-importance-of-transparent-communication.
6. Even government-classified secrets often stumble into the daylight. Just ask Julian Assange or Edward Snowden.

Chapter 8

1. Alicia Clegg, "The Myth of Authenticity," Bloomberg Businessweek, August 11, 2005, http://www.businessweek.com/stories/2005-08-11/the-myth-of-authenticity.
2. "Product & Company Information," Baileys website, accessed August 5, 2014, http://www.baileys.com/product-and-company-information/.
3. "Heritage Series. Handmade in Hope, Arkansas," Klipsch website, accessed August 5, 2014, http://www.klipsch.com/heritage-speakers.
4. Lydia Dishman, "No Bull*$@ Branding: How Companies

Use Trash Talk, Honesty to Charm the Right Customers," *Fast Company*, February 12, 2014, http://www.fastcompany. com/3026282/how-to-be-a-success-at-everything/no-bull-branding-how-companies-use-trash-talk-to-charm-the.

5. Ibid.

6. "Klipsch," *The Review Basket*, accessed September 16, 2014, http://www.netedge.co.in/sbd. aspx?bid=9916fa6a-3ec2-4fcc-ab40-56fe70cf5c50.

7. Simon Sinek, "People Seek Authenticity Even If They Can't Easily Define It," Fleishman Hillard *True*, last updated August 4, 2014, http://fleishmanhillard.com/2013/04/true/ people-seek-authenticity-even-if-they-cant-easily-define-it/.

8. Ben Richardson, "Anthropologie: Small Business Branding Lessons from a Major Brand," *Content Equals Money* (blog), May 21, 2013, https://contentequalsmoney.com/ anthropologie-case-study/.

9. Sohrab Vossoughi, "How to Stand Out? Try Authenticity," Bloomberg Businessweek, May 28, 2008, http:// www.businessweek.com/stories/2008-05-28/ how-to-stand-out-try-authenticitybusinessweek-business-news-stock-market-and-financial-advice.

Chapter 9

1. Taffy Brodesser-Akner, "The New American Dream," *Spirit Magazine*, March 2014, 78.

2. "The Artisans," 80.

3. Ibid.

4. Sohrab Vossoughi, "How to Stand Out? Try Authenticity," Bloomberg Businessweek, May 28, 2008, http:// www.businessweek.com/stories/2008-05-28/ how-to-stand-out-try-authenticitybusinessweek-business-news-stock-market-and-financial-advice.

5. Maura McCarthy, "The Case for Sharing Company Secrets," *Inc.*, February 6, 2012, http://www.inc.com/

maura-mccarthy/give-your-customers-more-control.html.
6. Judith Aquino, "The 10 Most Successful Rebranding Campaigns Ever," *Business Insider*, February 10, 2011, http://www.businessinsider.com/10-most-successful-rebranding-campaigns-2011-2?op=1#ixzz2iP3WMDcz.

Chapter 10

1. Jill Coody Smits, "The Long View," *Spirit Magazine*, March 2014, 64.
2. Bruce Horovitz, "Millennials Spur Capitalism with a Conscience," *USA Today*, March 27, 2013, http://www.usatoday.com/story/money/business/2013/03/25/kindness-panera-bread-nordstrom-starbucks/1965183.
3. Adam Grant, *Give and Take* (New York: Penguin, 2013).
4. Stacy Conradt, "11 of the Best Customer Service Stories Ever," *Mentalfloss*, updated July 15, 2014, http://mentalfloss.com/article/30198/11-best-customer-service-stories-ever.
5. Ibid.; also Mary Beth Quirk, "Zappos CSR's Kindness Warms Our Cold Hearts," *Consumerist*, January 17, 2011, http://consumerist.com/2011/01/17/zappos-customer-service-reps-kindness-warms-our-cold-hearts/.
6. Eddie Yoon, "The Generosity Strategies That Help Companies Grow," *Harvard Business Review Blog* Network, May 2, 2013, http://blogs.hbr.org/2013/05/netflix-reported-another-great/.
7. Ibid.
8. Ibid.

Chapter 11

1. "Interface's History," Interface website, accessed August 5, 2014, http://www.interfaceglobal.com/Company/History.aspx.
2. Elaine Woo, "Mogul Made His Firm Model Green Business,"

LA Times, August 15, 2011, http://articles.latimes.com/2011/aug/15/local/la-me-ray-anderson-20110815.

3. Paul Vitello, "Ray Anderson, Businessman Turned Environmentalist, Dies at 77," *New York Times*, August 10, 2011, http://www.nytimes.com/2011/08/11/business/ray-anderson-a-carpet-innovator-dies-at-77.html?_r=0.

4. "Interface's Values Are Our Guiding Principles," Interface website, accessed August 5, 2014, http://www.interfaceglobal.com/Company/Mission-Vision.aspx.

5. "Our Progress," Interface website, accessed August 5, 2014, http://www.interfaceglobal.com/Sustainability/Our-Progress.aspx.

6. "Interface's Values Are Our Guiding Principles," Interface website, http://www.interfaceglobal.com/Company/Mission-Vision.aspx.

7. "Awards," Interface website, accessed August 5, 2014, http://www.interfaceglobal.com/Newsroom/Awards.aspx.

8. "A Letter from Tim Cook on Maps," Apple website, accessed August 5, 2014, https://www.apple.com/letter-from-tim-cook-on-maps/.

9. Susan Tardanico, "10 Traits of Courageous Leaders," *Forbes*, January 15, 2013, http://www.forbes.com/sites/susantardanico/2013/01/15/10-traits-of-courageous-leaders/.

10. Rick Badie, "Ray Christie Anderson, 77: Was a Respected Manufacturing Environmentalist," *Atlanta Journal-Constitution*, August 10, 2011, http://www.ajc.com/news/news/local/ray-christie-anderson-77-was-a-respected-manufactu/nQKbD/.

11. Ibid.

Break the System for "Good"

1. James O'Toole, "J.C. Penney CEO's Pay Slashed as Company Struggles," *CNN Money*, April 2, 2013, http://money.cnn.

com/2013/04/02/news/companies/jc-penney-ceo-pay/.
2. Michael Hiltzik, "CEO-to-Worker Pay Gap Is Obscene;
   Want to Know How Obscene?" *Los Angeles Times,*
   October 20, 2013, http://www.latimes.com/business/la-fi-
   hiltzik-20131020,0,770122.column#axzz2yPzioeeU.

Chapter 12

1. Bureau of Labor Statistics, "Consumer Expenditure Survey,"
   United States Department of Labor, accessed August 5, 2014,
   http://www.bls.gov/cex/.
2. Bruce Horovitz, "Millennials Spur Capitalism with a
   Conscience," *USA Today,* March 27, 2013, http://www.
   usatoday.com/story/money/business/2013/03/25/
   kindness-panera-bread-nordstrom-starbucks/1965183/.
3. Ibid.
4. Paul Chaney, "Word of Mouth Still Most Trusted Resource
   Says Nielsen; Implications for Social Commerce,"
   Digital Intelligence Today, April 16, 2012, http://
   digitalintelligencetoday.com/word-of-mouth-still-most-
   trusted-resource-says-nielsen-implications-for-social-
   commerce/.
5. Ed Keller, "Finally, Proof That Word of Mouth Isn't Just
   'Nice to Have,' But Drives Measurable ROI," MarketShare,
   December 2006, http://marketshare.com/insights/
   blog/302-finally-proof-that-word-of-mouth-isn-t-just-nice-
   to-have-but-drives-measurable-roi.

Chapter 13

1. Steve Strauss, "Ask an Expert: Top Trends in Small Business,"
   USA Today, October 14, 2013, http://www.usatoday.
   com/story/money/columnist/strauss/2013/10/06/
   top-trends-in-small-business-steve-strauss/2931837/.

Chapter 14

1. Maya Albanese, "How She Leads: Hannah Jones of Nike," *GreenBiz*, February 6, 2012, http://www.greenbiz.com/blog/2012/02/06/how-she-leads-hannah-jones-nike.
2. Ibid.

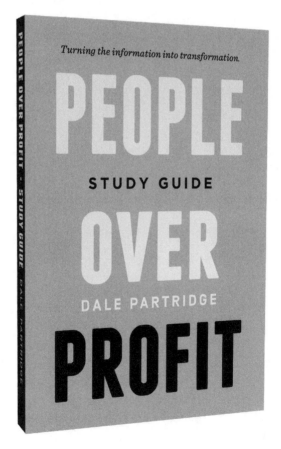